Such a rich tapestry of personal stories, clinical research, and Scripture woven into a very readable and insightful work, full of practical steps all of us can take. In *Beyond Burnout*, Amy O'Hana manages to handle complex concepts in a way that all of us can understand. It's as if she is in the room with you. Centered on the concept of "being," Amy makes you think and explore yourself in whole new ways, challenging you to "be." Simple, yet profound when understood. You owe it to yourself to dig in.

Bob Black
personal advisor and author of *Unlock Your Life:
5 Steps and a Jump to Living the Adventure God Made You For*

For the faith-based professional experiencing vocational burnout in the pursuit of fulfilling their life's purpose— or those who find themselves valiantly working to support their family—*Beyond Burnout* is salve to the soul. Thank you, Amy O'Hana, for your wisdom, understanding, and humor in this practical, hands-on approach to neutralizing burnout with a call to stillness.

Amy Turner
CEO and business coach, The Courage Tribe

Beyond Burnout

Amy O'Hana, PhD

HARVEST HOUSE PUBLISHERS
EUGENE, OREGON

Beyond Burnout
Copyright © 2020 by Amy O'Hana, PhD
Published by Harvest House Publishers
Eugene, Oregon 97408
www.harvesthousepublishers.com

ISBN 978-0-7369-8097-5 (pbk.)
ISBN 978-0-7369-8098-2 (eBook)

Library of Congress Cataloging-in-Publication Data

Names: O'Hana, Amy, author.
Title: Beyond burnout / Amy O'Hana, PhD.
Description: Eugene, Oregon : Harvest House Publishers, [2020]
Identifiers: LCCN 2020018961 (print) | LCCN 2020018962 (ebook) | ISBN 9780736980975 (pbk.) | ISBN 9780736980982 (eBook)
Subjects: LCSH: Burn out (Psychology) | Job stress. | Work--Psychological aspects. | Mental health--Religious aspects.
Classification: LCC BF481 .O48 2020 (print) | LCC BF481 (ebook) | DDC 158.7/23--dc23
LC record available at https://lccn.loc.gov/2020018961
LC ebook record available at https://lccn.loc.gov/2020018962

This book is dedicated to you, friend.
At the end of a long day or during a long season,
may you find rest in these pages.

Acknowledgments

To the One who breathes within me creativity and fervor, thank you for these words. May this book be your message, and may I be your scribe.

Steve Harper. Despite the demands of your graduate studies, you made space to support this project. Thank you for your research efforts and our green-tea conversations. You are the crown that surrounds this book with authenticity and depth.

Abby Kelley. You said yes to formatting at such a late date, and you did it all Chicago with a smile on your face and joy in your heart. Your light and energy are infectious. Thank you for your help.

To the amazing people at Harvest House—editors, designers, marketing, and sales—what a team you are! Gene Skinner, I love working with you. I so appreciate your suggestions and insights. Heather Green, you are always so upbeat and encouraging. Thank you for investing in me. Hope Lyda, your gift of friendship and wisdom of craft has meant the world to me. I have learned so much from all of you.

To those interviewed and represented throughout the book, thank you. I see your struggle, and it has *meant something*. Your vulnerability and your stories will encourage many. None of it was in vain.

Chris Cleaver, my dear friend. You held my heart through this entire process, and I will never forget it. Thanks for your critical eye and theological guidance. Solidarity to infinity and beyond!

To Dr. Dale-Elizabeth Pehrsson, my mentor and dissertation advisor at Oregon State University—thank you for your support those years ago. I will always remember you as one of my best teachers.

To my little Violet, the thought of watching you grow into your calling fueled my energy to finish this book. You can do anything you set your mind to do. But more than anything, I hope you learn to *be*.

Contents

A Note from the Author

In the years between earning my PhD and writing this book, I felt as if workforce stressors didn't change a lot. Sure, there were the normal fluctuations in the labor market, new jobs generated as a result of changing technology, and the like, but we've been aware of those for some time. However, between the completion of this manuscript and its publication, COVID-19 spun the world of work into a radical and unexpected crisis.

Talk about weird timing! In a short span, everything changed. From the ceasing of morning commutes, to running a business using Zoom or WebEx, to attempting to teach algebra to middle school kids—all from the dining room table! It was the ultimate recipe for burnout.

Four weeks into my self-quarantine, I experienced burnout like never before. I was exhausted from the never-ending crisis management prompted by the constant updates on the coronavirus. I had to work—I had to get things done. Except nothing was working.

As it turned out, I became one of the best case studies for my own book.

Through God's grace, however, staying at home turned out to be a blessing in disguise. Once I found a rhythm, I realized that my new schedule allowed time for deep contemplation about my work. What was important to me? What changes was I now forced to make as a result of a changing workplace? What changes did I need to make in my life vocation?

Admittedly, it was hard to take my own advice. But through the circumscribed stillness of the corona season, God taught me that staying at home is different from returning home. Home is not a place; it is not an address. *Home is a state of being.* It is a state of familiarity and stability, woven together in peace.

Home is the place to reconnect with the things and people you love, and to experience deep communion with Jesus.

Like mine, your work probably changed drastically in 2020 as a result of COVID-19, aggravating the burnout that was already there. What if your burnout is actually your divine stay-at-home order? Can you return home, to the place that you *know*, your place of stillness? God meets you everywhere, especially in your most frustrated, tired places. But he's there at home, setting out a fantastic dinner on the dining room table, waiting in anticipation for your return.

Stay home.

In grace and peace,

Amy

Dear Friend…

What happened?

You used to be happier and healthier. Now puffiness has trekked all over your face and the warmth has drained out of your eyes. And you are…so very tired.

I see you thumbing through these pages at your local bookstore or perhaps clicking through the contents online. You're longing for something that fills your emptiness—something to refresh the energy you once had. I know this title is probably piquing a dilemma within, even in these first few moments. On one hand, something in your heart responded to the cover. But on the other hand, a cynical snicker is bubbling up. *Who does this woman think she is, giving me solutions for my life?*

That's a reasonable question to ask. After all, you have it all together. You're a high achiever. A leader. A compassionate caretaker. You're the one who signs the checks, approves the budgets, delegates the tasks, makes the decisions, and cleans up the messes. You're the one who has the solution for everyone else's life.

But now your fire is burning out. Your energy is smoldering, just like the campfire on your family vacation last summer. (The campfire you didn't enjoy anyway because you were thinking about work—or maybe even working remotely.) Worse yet, you're no longer sure about your calling. The Voice that was once so clear feels silent. It's hard to admit—scary even—that you might be entering a spiritual and existential crisis.

You want to get back to the old you. The person who got things done. The person who was confident, who woke joyfully to greet each day with purpose and passion.

That's why I wrote this book.

I know what burnout is. I wrote an entire doctoral dissertation about it. I'm a professional woman, an educator, a mental health and vocational counselor, and a devout Christ-follower. And in addition to having a lot of book-learning about burnout, I've experienced it myself.

God healed me, and he showed me a way to restore others experiencing burnout. There is abundant life waiting for you. A life of connection and fulfillment—the life that Jesus had in mind for us all (John 10:10). Let's find that life together.

Introduction

Beginning a Conversation

The mind wants a job and loves to process things. The key to stopping this game is, quite simply, peace, silence, or stillness.

RICHARD ROHR, *THE NAKED NOW*

M ost adults are familiar with the word "burnout." In fact, when I asked people about the topic during the writing of this book, almost everyone chuckled and said, "Hey, do you need a case study?" I chuckled too because as a professional woman, I experienced burnout personally and witnessed it widely in the workplace. It's a frustrating experience, yet we bond together in our common understanding of it.

The term "burnout" originated in the 1970s by Manhattan psychoanalyst Dr. Herbert Freudenberger. While supervising counselors who work with people dealing with addiction, he noticed symptoms of emotional and physical fatigue that were impairing their work. He began referring to these individuals as "burnouts." The term caught on, and today we refer to occupational or vocational burnout.

Burnout affects a vast majority of the workforce, both in the United States and worldwide. Most adults will probably experience burnout at some point in their careers. To emphasize that fact, the World Health Organization (WHO) included "Burn-out" in the eleventh edition of the International Classification of Diseases (ICD-11) in 2019. Whoa! This means your *burnout thing* is serious. Health professionals now recognize burnout as an occupational phenomenon that warrants attention and treatment, and so should you.

If you find yourself chronically fatigued, unable to concentrate, cynical, and feeling your productivity slip, you are not alone. These symptoms are what constitute the common definition of burnout. But the root of burnout goes much deeper than workplace stress. There are many, many more factors that determine why and how we experience burnout. It is a complex interplay of external factors (your environment) and internal factors (your personal characteristics and experiences) that manifest uniquely in each person and situation. Mentioned less frequently are the deeper questions of meaning, fulfillment, and passion, but they play a significant role in your burnout as well.

Christian workers face additional challenges in their experience of burnout. Awareness of their vocational calling and a desire to please God through work adds additional pressure to perform. Those who have been taught traditional gender roles may face additional spiritual or existential dilemmas in their work. In career counseling, I've discovered that women and men have unique experiences in the workforce, so their experience with burnout can be a little different. That's why this book addresses work issues specific to women and to men. You'll find information based on current social norms, so please consider it a place to start a conversation rather than to end one. Through self-reflection and conversation with others, you'll have an opportunity to learn what's right for you.

A wide range of resources on burnout is available on the market today. You've probably already found quite a few titles that provide solutions to help your burnout, address burnout issues specific to certain careers, and more. What's missing is a tool that integrates Christian theology with research, experience, and suggestions you can try today. What's missing is an honest discussion of burnout's bottom line: disconnection from everything that is important to you, including your very heart and soul. What's missing is a tool that will compassionately walk you through some hard truths and help you make some hard decisions. Friend, that's what I'm hoping this book will be for you.

The good news? Those of us who have experienced burnout can be restored. You do not have to live or work in a burned-out state any longer. We will explore five intentions of burnout resolution, all of which occur step-by-step:

1. I will practice stillness so God can restore my soul.

2. I will seek connection with God, myself, and my work.

3. I will cultivate awareness of who I am, where I am, and what I want to be.

4. I will take consistent steps to promote well-being in my work.

5. I will focus on who I am to *be*, not what I am to *do*.

Along the way, you'll reconnect with God, yourself, and your work. Your heart will fill once again with love-energy for work, transforming your daily grind into so much more.

In chapter 1, we'll look at the beginning and end of burnout and consider our first restoration intention—stillness. Turn the page, and let's begin!

1

Be Beckoned

His banner over me is love.

SONG OF SONGS 2:4

I could see him across the room, slumped over the table like a benched football player who had taken more hits on the field than he could handle. An empty 24-ounce Starbucks cup was sitting near his notebook, and he was nursing a new cup of coffee provided by our work training facilitator. The crumbs in a Costco-sized muffin wrapper betrayed his carb-laden breakfast.

Mitchell was a work friend. We had finished our master's degrees in counseling and had begun working at the same community mental health agency. In our late twenties, we were idealistic and ready to save the world. Both Christians, we felt a strong spiritual calling to help others.

We had met a year ago in the agency's human resources training on our very first day of work. That day was fun. Mitchell was gregarious and outgoing, the kind of guy who made friends with everyone the instant they met. We had shared interests in our therapeutic work—we both wanted to help children experiencing trauma. He had just moved to the area with his wife, who had gotten her first professional job as an accountant. I had just finished graduate school and purchased my first home—the fulfillment of a lifelong dream. The future was bright, and we were both optimistic. After years of intense preparation for our careers, it was all going to pay off.

But today, Mitchell was slumped over.

I sought him out at break. "Hey, friend, how are you doing?"

He looked at me blankly, almost as if he couldn't recognize me. The smile that usually flashed so quickly barely cracked open his lips.

"Fine. Hangin' in," he replied.

I studied his face. I didn't see him that often anymore because we worked in different branches of the agency and had different supervisors. He had gained weight since our first day. Streaks of gray were already beginning to bud around his temples. His skin was faded yellow, and gray bags surrounded his eyes, pinching them so much it was hard to see that the warmth had bled out from them. But I noticed.

"Let's grab lunch," I said.

We scooted out to the Chinese place around the corner. Over pork fried rice, I gently but insistently asked him to tell me the truth. I was concerned about my friend and about his ability to work with his clients. I was also curious—how could Mitchell have changed so much in a year?

The truth wasn't pretty.

"I'm depressed, Amy." Shame began to creep over his face. "My doctor put me on medication. I never feel good anymore, and I don't want to get out of bed. I'm angry all the time. And my wife...we're having problems. She's threatened to leave if we don't go to counseling. I'm embarrassed to be in this situation—after all, I'm a counselor."

He told me everything. It was emotionally hard for him to work with children who were abused. His supervisor was unsupportive at best and mean at worst. With a high caseload, he felt like he could never get anything done. He was so exhausted when he got home, he couldn't engage his wife or friends. All of this was hard to hear, but somehow, I already knew. I had watched him slowly go downhill over the past year.

I completely understood what Mitchell was experiencing. Even though I wouldn't admit it, I was feeling the same way. My compassionate heart was becoming tightly knotted in cynicism. My clients' pain exhausted me, and I was beginning to question whether I still wanted to be a professional counselor. Evenings and weekends were spent looking for an out—either finding a different job or going back to school.

We were just one year into our careers. Something was very wrong with Mitchell, and something was very wrong with me. He was just having a harder time hiding it.

Crash and Burn

Mitchell's experience is more common than we'd like to admit. Idealistic with passion, energy, and calling, we set out to save the world—or at least to make a paycheck doing something meaningful. We're caught off guard when we crash and burn. The fervor that once burned so hot, so bright, eventually exhausts itself into smoldering embers.

It's scary and confusing because that's not what we expect from our careers. After all, if we are Christians who are walking in God's plan, everything should be great. Right?

I'm sure you've heard the word "burnout" before, especially in the workplace. It's like a tattoo stamped right over the nameplate on your office door—sometimes almost like a badge of honor. You've probably referred to being burned out yourself or suspected it about your coworkers. But what is burnout, really?

Researchers generally agree on three main characteristics of burnout: *Emotional exhaustion.* Once a loving and compassionate person, you are now devoid of feeling. Your heart literally cannot care anymore—or at least not nearly as much as it once did. In fact, caring for others or providing for them has become a chore, and that can lead to you feeling very resentful. When you experience emotional exhaustion, you can become cynical and sarcastic. Hope, joy, and optimism are replaced with macabre humor. This style of interpersonal relating and communication becomes a coping mechanism to protect your heart from holding more pain than it was intended to hold.

Physical exhaustion. You used to be in better physical health, but now your body doesn't work the way it used to. You are so very tired, probably because your sleep is disturbed by racing thoughts or you wake up too early every morning. You are likely gaining weight, especially around your torso. Because you are exhausted, your exercise and nutrition regimen slips, which creates a craving for quick-energy foods—sugar, caffeine, and simple carbs. And because you don't have the energy you once had, your productivity is slipping. You can't get things done the way you used to—maybe you can't even get to work on time anymore! It's hard to concentrate, and so you grab one more doughnut to get through the afternoon.

Loss of meaning. This is perhaps the key distinguishing feature of burnout, and it affects Christians just as much as anyone else. Your achievements and accomplishments don't feel good anymore, or they don't bring you the satisfaction you thought they would. You begin to doubt your calling, doubt your values, and doubt your dreams. Loss of meaning feels scary because it can create radical shifts in personality and behavior. People in this state may do things they never imagined they would do, such as develop addictions, have affairs, or engage in other unethical behavior.

Rest and Reconnect

Do you see any crash-and-burn symptoms in your life right now? Which ones? How are they affecting you and those you love?

Burnout Is About Work

Mitchell was suffering. He couldn't get out of bed, he had lost interest in things he loved, and he was irritable. It was affecting his productivity and marriage. As professional counselors, Mitchell and I both knew that his symptoms met diagnostic criteria for clinical depression.

But in actuality, Mitchell was not depressed. His symptoms began as a result of vocational stress, which distinguishes burnout from other mental and behavioral health issues. Burnout is always related to one's vocation or work life.

> Burnout is always related to one's vocation or work life.

This definition takes away a lot of stigma, doesn't it? It also helps us know where to start to fix it.

Burnout is often overlooked or misdiagnosed as another mental, emotional, or behavioral problem. But unless we name it correctly, we can't get to the root of the problem or focus our energy on helpful solutions. The good news is, when we identify burnout accurately and implement a restoration plan, we are much more likely to resolve it and avoid its long-term consequences.

Rest and Reconnect

Create a timeline of your work life. Identify points on the timeline where you first noticed signs of emotional exhaustion, physical exhaustion, and loss of meaning. If you've been diagnosed with depression or another mental disorder, is there any link between the onset of your symptoms and the distress in your work life?

Are You a Human Doing?

Whatever you do, work at it with all your heart, as working for the Lord, not for human masters, since you know that you will receive an inheritance from the Lord as a reward (Colossians 3:23-24).

How often do you feel as if you need to do more, to do better? This attitude is all around us—on social media, in the workplace, and even at church.

You're probably familiar with the verse above. As a type A high achiever, I've lived with this verse running on a loop in my head. Christians believe that work should please God instead of pleasing humans. A wonderful principle, yes, but it's not so wonderful when we focus only on "working" and not on "for the Lord."

The promise of a reward is enticing. If you work harder, do more—perhaps if you complete everything that has been assigned to you—then a reward in heaven will be waiting for you. When you achieve a goal, when you are a diplomatic boss or a caring parent, when you receive earthly accolades, ultimately, God is glorified. It's an honor...until it isn't. Because when you focus too much on all those great things, you can lose your focus on God and how much he loves you just as you are. When that happens—when you desire to please God in your work—he feels less like an adoring lover and more like a slave driver. You feel less like his beloved and more like his possession.

> When we are disconnected, we begin to equate our identity with achievement and performance rather than accepting and loving ourselves as the people God created us to be.

Have you ever met someone from a foreign country? What are the first questions they asked you as you became acquainted? They probably asked if you are married, have children...they wanted to know about your family and your friendships. That's because in many countries, a person's identity comes from his or her relationships. In contrast, in America, we often get acquainted by asking each other what we do for work. Sometimes we don't even ask about family relationships. In fact, in some work environments, asking about family relationships is taboo. American identity comes from what we *do*.

The focus on doing creates disconnection deep within. We begin to equate our identity with achievement and performance rather than accepting and loving ourselves as the people God created us to be. When we do not know who we really are, we have problems forming and maintaining quality relationships, and we disconnect even more. This leads to a vicious cycle of performance, disconnection, and renewed fervor to even higher performance, ultimately resulting in increased disconnection. Eventually, emptiness and exhaustion drive us to burnout.

God didn't create you to be a human doing. He created you as a human being to be in relationship with him and with others and to advance love in the world. Your unique purpose was formed by this divine intention.

Rest and Reconnect

If your desire to please God in your work was more about *someone to be* and less about *something to do*, how might your life look different? If you're struggling with this concept, don't worry—we will revisit it in chapter 14.

Before You Make Any Decisions

Mitchell was experiencing a lot of personal difficulty, and so were the people in his life. Your burnout reaches far beyond you. If you are tired and cranky and can't go out and do stuff like you used to, how can you possibly partner in meaningful relationships?

And what about the people you care for? When you are burned out, they suffer too. I once had a supervisor ask, "Do you not care enough about your clients to be your very best self for them?" Whoa...reality check! If I was going to be effective in my work, I had to take care of myself. Self-care was not a luxury; it was an ethical priority.

Mitchell and his wife were on the verge of a separation. At the time, they felt their marital stress intensely, but the focus of it was displaced. By all accounts, it seemed like their marital stress was based on Mitchell's failure to engage. But the deeper, unaddressed problem was Mitchell's lack of self-care. The relationship distress was really a symptom of a bigger problem.

Are you currently experiencing a crisis, or are you quickly headed there? I invite you to read this book completely before you make any permanent decisions, such as getting divorced or quitting your job. If burnout is the core issue, the crisis will resolve once you find restoration. At the very least, it will become much easier to handle.

> Self-care is not a luxury; it is an ethical priority.

If you suspect someone you love is burned out, this book will be a great tool to gain insight into their experience. You don't have to take your loved one's burnout issues personally; this is their responsibility to address. But you will learn how to support your loved one through restoration.

Rest and Reconnect

Who or what else outside of yourself has been affected by your burnout? In what ways?

Beyond Burnout: Where You're Headed

I'm going to ask you to do something unconventional. Something that all your teachers said you should *never* do when reading a book and something that might make my publishers shake their heads.

I'd like you to read the last chapter first.

Why? Because it's important to begin with the end in mind. I want you to know exactly where you're headed in your journey of healing. It's an absolutely hopeful and beautiful place, and it will give you context as you read the rest of this book. So turn to page 203. I'll be waiting right here when you are done.

> Begin with the end in mind.

And now, welcome back to chapter 1. You might think, *Amy, thanks for that nice visual. I'd love ambient lights over a backyard BBQ and maybe even a 1978 Chevy...but that doesn't fix my burnout right now.*

Yes, I know. Believe me, if you feel like the crispy-charred gristle bits stuck to the bottom of that BBQ instead of the pulsating channel of God's love-energy for work, I can relate. I've felt like those gristle bits myself. Why do you think I wrote my doctoral dissertation on occupational burnout? The problem is, your heart was once filled with joy in your work. Perhaps now it feels more like a discarded wine barrel, empty and dry.

You want solutions, fast. You want to heal, to get through a workday without dreading every second of it. Because you have to work. Earning a paycheck isn't optional; you have responsibilities to take care of. You'd like to be able to enjoy each day at least a little rather than trying to think of excuses to call in sick when your alarm goes off.

Like Mitchell, maybe you are at a critical point. Perhaps you've made some poor choices, and you might stand to lose more than just a little sleep. It could be your job, your marriage, your finances, your health, your reputation...anything that has been touched by your emotional and physical exhaustion.

Maybe you've carried this burden for a long time. You can still find some meaning in your work, but it's hard. Your work is important, and you keep telling yourself, *This is just a season. I'll get through it.* But nothing has changed yet.

Or maybe you're considering leaving your work altogether. Someone else can balance the accounting sheets, preach the sermons, design the websites, splice the wires, or tend to the broken hearts or broken bodies. You're not sure what you will do—or whether you can actually leave.

There *is* a way to get to that backyard BBQ you read about in chapter 15, a way to get to those moments of satisfaction, joy, and peace. I wish it were as simple as reading the last chapter first, but it isn't. It's going to take some work on your part, and that's what we'll do in chapters 2–14. I promise this work won't feel like the work you do every day. This is personal, spiritual, and existential work. It might be a little painful at times, but since you were courageous enough to reach for this title, I know you have the gumption to finish it. And when you reach chapter 15 again—wow, it will hold so much more meaning.

I'll be with you every step of the way. We will make a great team!

When I was burned out, the last thing I needed was another thing to do. So I've written this book as an experience—a pathway to *be* and to reconnect. You will learn some facts about burnout, but more importantly, you'll have opportunities to take time out and rest. Each chapter is designed for you to take in slowly and reflectively. I've titled each one with language to emphasize *being* rather than *doing*. I invite you to have something to write with as you read. Don't rush through this; take your time. Rest and reconnect.

At the end of each chapter, you'll find a short exercise to help you be still with God and also a page where you can create a to-be list. There are no to-do lists in this book. God knows a to-do list is the last thing you need right now—literally! This book is a perfect companion for a well-deserved vacation or a great way to start a sabbatical. Bonus points if you stop right now and plan your next getaway...even if it's a staycation.

Give your rational mind a rest and let your heart lead. Reconnect deeply with things that are important to you, beginning with your relationship with God. When you reconnect with God's voice, his passionate love for you, and his good intention for you, things change.

Be Beckoned

When your heart is empty, you crave something to replenish it. In fact, that's how you get into trouble; an empty heart will open to anything it perceives will fill it. That's just the way God created you. Your heart is designed to be filled by relationship and connection.

You are waiting, lonely, longing for a lover to find you. A lover to see you. A lover to bring you into relationship.

Your Lover is here now.

It was this Voice that first called you. The Voice that first filled your heart with passion, energy, and vocation. The Voice that told you about meaning, productivity, and fulfillment.

It's always been there. And it's still here, beckoning.

Your Lover sees your empty heart and wants to unravel its knots of cynicism or despair. To hold you and heal you. You don't have to *do* anything for this love. You are the receiver. Simply by being alive, by being here, you can receive it. Love is here. Restoration is here.

Your Lover is beckoning. Open your heart and receive.

Chapter 1 Key Points

- Burnout looks like depression and comes solely from your work or vocation.

- A mentality of achievement and performance creates a deep sense of disconnection.

- God is beckoning. He wants to refresh your heart with passion and purpose for work.

Practice Being Beckoned

Be still with God. Remove any distractions that may be present. Sit or lie comfortably, close your eyes, and open your hands. Allow God's Spirit to fill your heart, body, and mind. Stay in this moment as long as you can. When finished, journal briefly about this experience. What happened? What came to your awareness?

This Week's To-Be List

The Five Intentions of Burnout Resolution

I.
I will practice stillness so God can restore my soul.

II.
I will seek connection with God, myself, and my work.

III.
I will cultivate awareness of who I am, where I am, and what I want to be.

IV.
I will take consistent steps to promote well-being in my work.

V.
I will focus on who I am to *be*, not what I am to *do*.

2

Be Longing

Hope deferred makes the heart sick, but
a longing fulfilled is a tree of life.

PROVERBS 13:12

et's play volleyball!" My friend Belinda's voice was mischievous despite the impending raindrops from the gray clouds sneaking over the August sun.

"Umm..." I said, "isn't it a little cold?"

I didn't even try to hide my ambivalence. I'm usually up for volleyball, but my friend wanted me to play over the net staked in the shallows of Cultus Lake. The lakes in the mountains of central Oregon are *cold*, even in the summer. Though the water would only reach my knees, I knew goosebumps would explode all over my body the minute my toes touched the water.

"Come on," she said. "We've already been in, and we have plenty of time before the storm hits."

She was right. We had spent the day on Jet Skis and paddleboards in celebration of her daughter's birthday. As professional women, we were rarely able to enjoy lazy summer Tuesdays like this. Perhaps I just needed to get over myself and get into the water.

I put my right foot in. *Ugh*—it was cold.

With a hesitant swoosh of water, my left foot joined my right. I was determined to do this even though I was already chilled. It would be worth it to have a bit more fun before packing it in for the day. I began walking out to the net, and Belinda sent a volley straight over. I lunged and...

SPLASH! Missed it.

Well, forget about maintaining warmth and a sense of decorum fitting a professional woman! I was soaked head to toe and shaking from the blasts of cold air hitting my body. I was also embarrassed. There was nothing left to do but laugh—and play.

And play we did. We were both soaked from the splashing and the raindrops slowly starting to fall. We didn't even notice. Soon we abandoned the traditional spike, set, and bump and simply tossed the ball over the net. Like the volleyball, our words bounced back and forth as we shared about work, love, kids, our worries and fears, and our hopes and dreams.

That day is one of my happiest memories of being with Belinda.

Is Happiness Your Goal?

I'm going to suggest something radically unconventional—something that flies in the face of the cultural status quo. Are you ready? You may well be burned out in part because you are trying too hard to be happy.

Umm, what? Amy, happiness is a good thing. How could I burn out from trying to be happy?

Happiness is a desirable state; some would say it's one of the highest goals possible. Thousands of books on happiness are available. You can choose from an endless supply of workshops and flood your inbox and smartphone with thousands of motivational sayings, blogs, podcasts, Pinterest pins...you get the idea. We want happy. *You* want happy.

I used to think happiness is all I wanted too, especially in the seasons when I didn't feel particularly happy. But a while back, I had an aha moment...

If happiness is your goal, then it's something you're working for.

Now, don't get me wrong. Happiness is a fantastic goal, and having goals are what move you toward getting what you want. Achieving goals gives us a sense of satisfaction. But misdirected goals can lead straight to...you guessed it: burnout.

Rest and Reconnect

A psychologist named C.R. Snyder developed a concept called hope theory.[1] He believed hope to be not only an emotion but also a way of thinking. In other words, hope comes from the mind as well as the heart. Snyder's work confirmed that people with higher hope have better life outcomes.

According to Snyder, two things help us have hope that we will achieve our goals: pathway thinking and agency thinking. Pathway thinking is the ability to envision routes to your goals. Agency thinking is the motivation to use those routes and achieve your goals. Consider these three exercises:

- Use some time in thoughtful prayer and reflection to identify one goal that is important to you. (You probably have lots of them, but just choose one for now.)
- List some pathways—some steps you can take—that will lead you toward that goal.
- Identify some ways you can build your agency—your motivation and determination to overcome obstacles and achieve your goal. Don't worry if this is difficult right now. The following chapters will give you clarity about agency.

Consider this principle: "Hope deferred makes the heart sick, but a longing fulfilled is a tree of life" (Proverbs 13:12). This proverb is talking about hope that is set aside or not fully realized. Without hope, you would never set a goal in the first place. Without hope, you would never move toward a goal. You never would have trained for your career, let alone shown up at a job interview, if you didn't have hope! But when hope is not actualized to its fullest, eventually your heart doesn't have the energy and vitality it once had. Something feels terribly wrong.

The Shallow Side of Hope

I wouldn't say playing volleyball with Belinda was a goal. I never wrote down "play volleyball in knee-deep water" on my to-do list or motivational board. Instead, my goals included "have more fun" and "rest this summer." I certainly achieved those goals. But my happiness soon wore off. In fact, it wore off during the 25-minute drive home from the lake. Already I was preoccupied with what I needed to accomplish next and how I could have more fun the next day.

Happiness is awesome, but it's a short-term deal. That's why Proverbs 13:12 says hope deferred makes the heart sick. Hope is good, but when you put it aside, or when it is consummated by achievement, you need something else to sustain your energy and move you forward.

That something else is fulfillment.

Fulfillment is similar to achievement in that it produces a planned-for or desired outcome. Have you ever heard the statement "I fulfilled my promise"? It means that a debt was paid or an agreement was met. But to the human soul, fulfillment runs much deeper than achievement.

Psalm 71:5 says, "You have been my hope, Sovereign LORD, my confidence since my youth." This verse describes hope as a decision followed by a long-lasting pursuit. Sort of like Snyder's hope theory: an intention, action, and determination. But the psalmist doesn't talk about goals or the ups and downs of life. He doesn't need to because of his deep and trusting relationship with God.

Fulfillment is open to both the good and the bad, accepting of whatever God gives and allows. It is contentment with what *is* while working toward what is *not yet*. It is attained through the pursuit of connection and relationship with God, yourself, your community, and your work. It lasts a lot longer than happiness. Fulfillment is hope actualized to its fullest. It sometimes includes happiness, but it always rises above it.

> Fulfillment sometimes includes happiness but always rises above it.

Happiness is the fun, shallow version of hope. It's me standing knee-deep in the water in front of the volleyball net because I wanted to enjoy and challenge myself. Fulfillment is the more substantial and deeper version of hope. It's me diving into the water after that darn ball, getting soaked, and then laughing hysterically with Belinda about how ridiculous we both must have looked. The memory we'll share forever meets a need in my heart for friendship, trust, and connection.

The Deepest Side of Hope

I've been a mental health counselor for almost 20 years. I have yet to have a counseling client say, "I want to feel more fulfilled." Instead, they usually say, "I want to be happy," or "I want to feel less anxious."

All clients *know* that something is just...off. Perhaps they can't articulate what it is, but they know something deeper is driving them to counseling. We counselors refer to this experience as "existential angst," which is a questioning of the meaning of one's life or life itself. In healthy situations, existential angst prompts clients to undergo deep self-examination and then make decisions that lead to transformed lives. In unhealthy situations, existential angst can bring deep despair or hopelessness.

God has a different name for existential angst: longing. Consider the second part of Proverbs 13:12: "Hope deferred makes the heart sick, but a longing fulfilled is a tree of life." Longing is a dull ache; it's something you are just barely aware of. It's what you feel in the dead of night when quietness unlocks the floodgates of thoughts and feelings resting just under the surface. It's a deep desire to engage with someone or something you love. It's a desire to feel complete.

Longing makes us uncomfortable, but God didn't create longing to torment us. Not at all. Instead, he created longing as a pathway to our fulfillment. Longing is a gift to drive us, to teach us, and to move us toward deeper relationships. Without it, we would have little motivation to move toward fulfillment. Instead, we would be content with happiness, only accomplishing the things in our day-to-day lives.

But in his fullness and because of his fullness, God wants us to also experience fullness.

Fulfillment is connected to your soul, which is the eternal part of you that is created in the image of God. The soul is separated from God in this existence and deeply longs to return to him or reconnect with him. Fulfillment is cultivated by discovering—or remembering—the very essence of who God created you to be. This book won't tell you what your personal fulfillment looks like. No book can. Your fulfillment will be unique and personal, requiring the search, examination, and possibly the uprooting of your very soul.

But sojourner, be warned. Since this journey is rooted in the soul, it is indeed soul work. Deep. Sometimes painful. Sometimes it means delaying happiness for something greater. Sometimes it includes deconstructing everything you ever believed in, only to reconstruct it according to God's leading.

Not an easy journey, but such a hopeful one. In fact, pursuing fulfillment is probably one of the most hopeful journeys on which you could ever embark. Like the hope expressed in Psalm 71:5, this journey begins with a decision of trust in Something Greater than you and your current situation.

Are you ready to put your foot in the water?

Rest and Reconnect

Spend a few moments in silence, prayer, meditation, or reflection on this question:

"God, what is your vision for my fulfillment?"

When you have that vision, spend some time journaling, doodling, drawing, singing, writing, or otherwise expressing it.

The Very First Verb

I imagine you could be feeling a bit of angst as you read this chapter. On top of the frustration and despair you might be feeling about your burnout, now you have yet another thing to do: Put aside happiness in pursuit of fulfillment. *Come on, Amy, please don't give me another thing to do!*

Here's the most hopeful message I have for you: Fulfillment is not something that goes on your to-do list. Because it's not a goal you achieve. It's a state of being that you cultivate over time. It's also a healing agent of burnout and the best way to prevent its return.

Imagine a beautiful garden filled with all kinds of fragrant flowers and tasty vegetables. The garden didn't start out that way. Someone tilled the earth and planted seeds...and then watered them, nurtured them, and tended to them. Yes, it took time and effort, as well as some messiness and pain. But oh, was it ever a labor of love. Was it ever something to delight in! Didn't it produce such pride and contentment after years of toil? A gardener who cultivates that kind of garden embraces the work with deep joy, love, and commitment.

Have you ever thought about tending to your personal fulfillment with the same joy, love, and commitment as that gardener? Even though the work is messy and dirty sometimes? God tends to us this way, and you can do so too. In fact, God is delighted when he sees you listening to the longing he planted deep in your soul.

You'll learn more about cultivating fulfillment throughout this book. For now, let's start with the very first step of cultivating fulfillment: *being*.

Being is your first identity—not doing, like our culture often teaches. Look at this verse:

> Then God said, "Let us make man in our image, in our likeness, so that they may rule over the fish in the sea and the birds in the sky, over the livestock and all the wild animals, and over all the creatures that move along the ground." So God created man in his own image, in the image of God he created them; male and female he created them (Genesis 1:26-27).

God created humans in his image—as beings—before assigning us work.

What is being? Did anyone ever teach you that concept or show you what it looked like? Probably not. Yet deep inside, you know. It is a present, conscious connection to your whole self, returning to the state of *what is* or *I am*. I'm sure you remember grammar lessons in elementary school. The *being* verbs ("am," "is," "are," "was," "were," "be," "being," "been") were the very first things you learned. You learn the verb "to be" first because just like sentence structure, being is the most foundational part of existence.

> **Fulfillment is a state of being that is cultivated over time.**

Be-Longing

> He refreshes my soul (Psalm 23:3).

Psalm 23 is one of my favorite passages in the Bible because it's such a wonderful picture of being. It's God—the Good Shepherd—seeking you, finding you, gathering you, holding you, and setting you back into a spacious place. There is no doing on your part; God is the one who does all the doing. Your job (no pun intended) is to simply be found.

Rest and Reconnect

Our first intention of burnout resolution has to do with slowing down: "I will practice stillness so God can restore my soul." Stillness is the first practical step toward *being* instead of *doing*. It is the intentional slowing down of the body and mind in order to open the heart to receive God's presence.

In burnout, your heart, body, and mind are hijacked. (You'll learn later in the book what actually hijacks them, but for now, just note that your burnout is in control, leaving you overwhelmed and powerless.) Stillness helps you reconnect to God's wisdom and voice. God always beckons you to be still, but he leaves it up to you to listen and actually do it. If the practice of stillness feels ambiguous or strange to you—have no fear! Here are three actions to help you practice:

First, slow your body and mind. Stillness allows your nervous system to rest. Thoughts and feelings pushed down during the busyness of the day will come to the surface. You will become aware of deeper things, including God's voice.

Take a minute right now to be still. Sit or lie down and slowly read or recite a Scripture that invites peace. I love Psalm 46:10: "Be still and know that I am God." You may choose to close your eyes, or you can leave them open. Breathe deeply. If your eyes are closed, focus your awareness on things you don't normally focus on, such as the sounds or smells around you or feelings that come up. If your eyes are open, choose to observe things that you find beautiful or that bring you joy. Notice them. Open your heart to God in gratitude for them.

Second, set your intention to be. Setting your intention means consciously choosing to move toward something or being open to receiving it. It's almost like planting a seed and watching it grow. When you set an intention to *be*, you are deciding to experience rather than do. Setting your intention is the only thing your mind needs to do right now.

In this moment of stillness, open your heart to receive God's love. Ask God to help you see yourself the way he sees you—worthy simply because you exist and because he created you, not because of what you do or produce. Open your heart to receive God's affirmation of who you are.

Third, allow. Allowing is a nonjudgmental experience of whatever comes up for you—good things, difficult things, and direction from the Holy Spirit. It is allowing God's presence to envelop you so that you can experience a deeper connection to the Divine.

Ask God to reveal what he wants to reveal to you right now, in this moment. If it's painful, simply observe it without judgment and then ask God to help you. If it's wonderful, receive it as a gift from him. In each case, ask God, "What do you want to show me about my fulfillment in this?"

You're not going to get all your answers today, and that's okay. Restoration is a process that happens over time. Continue to practice stillness, opening your heart to what God wants to teach you.

In all of God's doing and in all of your being, your soul is restored. Restoration is the peaceful return of your soul to its natural state—full, complete, and one with God. It is the most foundational, most natural, and most amazing experience you can imagine. It is what you were created for.

Your heart was created with a longing to *be*—a *be-longing*—with God.

Being is so important in your burnout restoration because it is the antithesis of doing. It comes naturally when you allow yourself to disconnect from the chaos, the "shoulds," and the crazy around you. It happens when you shift your focus away from *all the doing*. It happens when you are working from the intention to be who you authentically are—who God created you as and who he's called you to be. It is the big-picture view of your burnout resolution and vocational fulfillment.

You've been doing for a long time, and it's not working anymore. It's time to reconnect with the parts of you that have been lost or forgotten. Time to let work stay at work and no longer allow it to control your mind or interrupt your sleep. Time to enjoy your life without obsessing about your to-do list. Time to experience peace and fulfillment instead of nervous-system overstimulation every day.

> A state of being requires stillness. A state of doing requires action.

Restoration starts with *being*—the state your longing is leading you to.

Be still and pay attention to your *be*-longing.

It had been a while since I felt fulfilled, that day I played volleyball with Belinda. I had just come off a grueling summer quarter of teaching and writing. That afternoon, I experienced a connection that not only reenergized my body but also deeply restored my soul.

It was never about the volleyball, the Jet Skis, or the paddleboard. It wasn't that we felt rebellious or in control of our lives because we abandoned work that day. It was about our conversation, our openness to share our lives with each other. It was us *being* together. Because connection and relationship go hand in hand with fulfillment.

We'll unpack that idea more in chapter 3.

Chapter 2 Key Points

- Happiness is a worthy goal—in the short run. Fulfillment includes happiness but also transcends it.

- God tends to you with joy, love, and commitment. You honor God by tending to your fulfillment in the same way.
- *Being* is the first step on the pathway to fulfillment.

Practice Being

Practice stillness and *being*—with God. Remove any distractions that may be present. Sit or lie comfortably, close your eyes, and open your hands.

God, I trust that you have placed a longing in my heart that will lead me to fulfillment. Give me the courage to move toward abundant life—to tend to myself with the same joy, love, and commitment that you do.

This Week's To-Be List

_____

_____

_____

_____

_____

_____

_____

_____

_____

_____

_____

_____

_____

_____

3

Be Connected

*Then God said, "Let us make man
in our image, in our likeness."*

GENESIS 1:26

The other day, I had coffee with a colleague. She had recently earned
her PhD in counselor education and landed her dream job at a
prestigious university. It was a high-paying job on a tenure track.
I told her I was writing this book, and she asked me what I thought
caused burnout. I told her what the research said and that I believed
burnout is ultimately a result of disconnection.

Her eyes began welling with tears. She was working all the time,
putting in much longer hours than she did in graduate school. The job
required a move to a different state, a substantial plane flight away from
her friends and family. She loved animals but was spending more time
in a barn than developing her social life. Despite the great achievement
of finishing her education and landing her dream job, she felt a perva-
sive emptiness in everything she did.

She had never felt more disconnected in her life.

Craving Connection

Can you relate to my colleague's experience? Perhaps, like her, you worked hard to train for your career. Or perhaps you worked your way up the ladder and were finally offered a dream job. It was so exciting...for a while. But now you feel a deep emptiness that bleeds into all aspects of your life.

In chapter 2, we talked about longing. Longing is a spiritual thirst to engage with what brings you love and helps you feel complete. It's a gift from God that moves you toward fulfillment. But there's something else about longing that is quite poignant:

Longing always leads us to relationship because that's where we find love and completeness.

When I wrote my doctoral dissertation on occupational burnout, I wanted to find out exactly what caused it. But the literature is mixed. Some scholars believe burnout is caused by external factors, such as a high workload or insufficient supervision—usually the result of a poorly managed workplace.[1] Others believe it is caused by internal factors, such as personality styles or ineffective ways of coping.[2] My dissertation research found that both external and internal factors contributed to burnout. But there was no definitive confirmation as to what actually causes it.

How frustrating! If we don't know what causes burnout, how do we fix it?

I've done a lot of research and pondering about the root cause of burnout. In the years since I completed my dissertation, I've had the opportunity to counsel and teach working professionals. As a working professional myself, I've experienced seasons of fulfillment and seasons of burnout. And here's something I've observed over and over, something we absolutely must grasp before we can heal from burnout:

People crave connection.

Plugged In but Disconnected

Amy, the fact that people crave connection isn't news to me.

It doesn't seem like an earth-shattering principle, does it? You already know that people crave connection. You've experienced that craving, and I have too. Something about deep, authentic connection gives us a sense of belonging and purpose. It makes us feel alive.

When you are disconnected, you are empty. You exist, and the outside looks good—sometimes great, in fact. There is a clear shell of self-definition. But on the inside, there is no color, only dullness and an ache for light.

Connection is restored when people intentionally come together. Their protective shells soften and merge, creating a bond. Their weak hearts begin beating in time. The strength of that shared heartbeat fills their empty souls with the joyful sounds and vibrant colors of authentic relationships. In the pounding rhythm, strength pulsates through their bodies.

It's like blasting Ace of Base on your way to work. Pure energy.

Connection is one of the greatest human psychological needs.[3] As Christians, we know God created us for deep connection. Everything we do—every experience in life—is about connection. Even your work. *Especially* your work.

You may feel completely disconnected from your work right now. In fact, you may feel disconnected from a lot of things...or even everything.

It's one thing when your soul knows that a type of connection exists but has never experienced it. That's like a young person who looks forward to meeting the love of their life, knows it will happen eventually, but hasn't experienced it yet. That's a form of disconnection colored by longing. But a deeper, sadder form of disconnection occurs when a natural connection has been lost or retracted. When the vibrant colors of sunrises and sunsets fade to a consistent, dull gray...or even to darkness.

The ache, the longing that type of disconnection produces, is indescribable.

Friend, *this* is the color of burnout. A natural connection to your work or calling that has been lost or retracted. And now things just feel...so dark.

You undoubtedly started your career with a deep connection to your work; it gave you meaning in some form. Or you started a job with a connection to something—even if it was simply making a paycheck to support your family. But now that connection is gone. You are still plugged in, but you are disconnected.

You sure got that right, Amy. So how do I fix it?

Figure out how to get back to color from grayscale.

Rest and Reconnect

In relationship counseling, we refer to disconnection as a "rupture." To repair a rupture, you must return to the first point of disconnection. When a disconnection occurs, you are likely to find yourself on a slippery slope of misunderstanding and miscommunication. As you can imagine, this slippery slope leads straight to the destruction of the relationship. But if you can repair the disconnection, you have a greater chance of reconnecting, moving forward, and strengthening the relationship. Relationships that master this practice over time will mature, grow, and deepen in their connection and commitment.

Spend some time in thoughtful reflection on the following questions. Feel free to journal, draw, or doodle your process.

- What was the very first disconnection you experienced from work?
- What was happening at work? Who was there?
- What was happening in your life outside of work?
- If you could repair this disconnection, what would it look like? What would be the best possible outcome?
- What would you need to do within yourself to feel strong enough to repair it? Who would you need to talk to? Who would you solicit for support?

Serve Me Up a Big Plate of Lonely

I love football—maybe you do too. So if you will, imagine with
me for a moment an upcoming big game. A
really important game, like a conference championship or the Super Bowl. This is gonna be a
big deal, so you will be prepared. You shop and
you clean, you make sure you can stream ESPN,
and you hire a babysitter. Nothing is going to
stop you from enjoying this game!

> Burnout occurs
> when your
> connection to
> work has been
> lost or retracted.

On the day of the game, you get up early.
Because as we all know, one of the best things about a big game is,
well, the food. So you cook. And you cook. And you cook some more.
Nachos loaded with jalapeños and homemade cheese sauce. Chicken
wings baked in the oven and then crisped to perfection on the BBQ.
Beer (or kombucha) and peanut butter brownies. Plus a whole lot of
other things you've wanted to nosh for a while but haven't because you
are watching your waistline. You've got the tastiest spread in town, all
laid out in the dining room, finger-lickin' ready to enjoy while everyone cheers on their favorite team. And then...

No one comes over.

Were you so busy preparing that you forgot to invite anyone? Or
do none of your friends like football? No matter the reason, you are
left to watch the game alone.

How would that feel? If it were me, the sickness in my heart would
be worse than the sickness in my belly from all that food. I would feel
foolish for all the effort I had put into making the day special. And even
more painful, the loneliness of the moment would rob me of any satisfaction I may have experienced.

A wise king described this scenario so well:

> There was a man all alone; he had neither son nor brother.
> There was no end to his toil, yet his eyes were not con-
> tent with his wealth. "For whom am I toiling," he asked,

"and why am I depriving myself of enjoyment?" This too
is meaningless—a miserable business! (Ecclesiastes 4:8).

King Solomon, the wisest and wealthiest man of his age, knew that
everything—even a good thing, like our career—becomes meaningless if we can't enjoy it with someone. We want to share our labor and
the fruits of our labor with others. When our work brings them joy, we
share in that joy. It gives us pleasure to show others what we have pro-
duced and to care for them with it.

But even deeper, I think King Solomon knew that a lack of sharing
would rob us of connection. The end result? A big, awesome spread
with an even bigger spread of loneliness.

Sustained disconnection results in loneliness and strips you of
meaning. It is exactly the opposite of what God intended for your
existence. And yet I would venture to say that all of us have felt disconnected and lonely at some time.

Psychoanalyst Carl Jung said, "Loneliness does not come from having no people about one, but from being unable to communicate the
things that seem important to oneself, or from holding certain views
which others find inadmissible." Even though you may be a leader at
your workplace, have a spouse and family, or be a respected member
of your church or community, you can still be lonely. Loneliness is a
result of feeling like you cannot be who you are, or share things deeply
important to you, without being judged.

The antidote to loneliness? You already know what I'm going to say.
Authentic connection.

Transcend the Paycheck

Tim, a middle-aged man, stops by your office every day. He's been
a UPS driver since his early twenties. He carries a lighthearted joy and
humor along with his packages. He works efficiently and with purpose.
When he talks about his wife and boys, his face lights up like a small
child left to destroy a balloon arch with a safety pin.

Rest and Reconnect

From whom or what do you feel disconnected?

You may be disconnected from your relationship with God. God is the Ultimate Source, where we come from and what gives us life and energy. Sin, which is prompted by fear and pain, disconnects us from God. You long to come back to that connection with God, even if you are not consciously aware of it and even if you are not particularly religious. Disconnection from God creates loneliness in your soul. Soul loneliness is deeply existential, causing you to question your purpose in life and hindering you from finding meaning.

You may be disconnected from your relationship with yourself. Sometimes we struggle with knowing who we are or who God created us to be. Thus you become who or what you think you *should* be as defined by the outside world. Disconnection with the self makes you feel lonely in your heart. You may struggle with expressing yourself fully and living an authentic life because you are concerned with acceptance or maintaining the status quo.

You may be disconnected from your relationship with work. You may have never considered that you have a relationship with work...you may have always assumed that it is a natural part of life, so just get to it! But whatever you engage with, you also have a relationship with. Disconnection from work makes you feel lonely in your mind. You know you have much to contribute, but burnout may make you question what you are doing and why you are doing it. Soon, it is difficult to concentrate or be as productive as you once were.

You may feel disconnection in any or all of these areas. What do you need to reconnect these relationships?

Was Tim's great purpose in life to be a UPS driver? Perhaps. I've known Tim personally since we were teens. He's always loved driving. He's always loved people too, and what better job to make people happy than delivering packages?

Authentic connection is a necessity for healthy relationships.

But my suspicion is that Tim finds a deeper meaning in his work. It is clear that what he does every day blesses not only the people around him but also his family—one of his deepest values. His wife stays at home and takes care of their two sons. They are able to make it financially with one income living in Portland, Oregon, because of Tim's work ethic and stellar employment history.

Tim's work is not just about a paycheck. It's not even about the tasks he performs. It's about people—his family and customers. His job is just a piece of his life—one piece of a greater whole. He's found a way to transcend the daily grind through authentic connection.

Tim is one of the most fulfilled men I know. Loneliness? Not even in his vocabulary.

A Great Gestalt

Oneness is another word for connection. God made us for oneness—he is one, and he made us in his image. We are made for union, for relationships with God and each other. Oneness is the model for all our relationships—with our intimate partners, with our families and friends, and in our communities.

As Christians, we are taught that relationship with God is ultimately what fulfills us. But Christian teaching often misses this important point: Your relationship with God is not the only thing you long for. The longing for connection is present across all aspects of your being. You also long for oneness with whomever or whatever you share relationship.

Rest and Reconnect

What is healthy authenticity? Does it mean you show up to a professional office in your yoga pants or write an angry email because that's "authentic"? I'm not sure such a display would work out very well in the long run. In fact, I think it would eventually lead to disconnection and alienation.

Healthy authenticity should always be about relationship. In relationship, there is a "you," a "me," and a "we." Unfortunately, sometimes we miss the "you" and "we" parts of the relationship. When you do or say whatever you want, expressing only the self and without intending to move toward relationship, you have the potential to do great damage. Instead, if you can learn to fully express yourself *and* fully hear others, committing to work together toward a mutually beneficial relationship, you will foster connection in a safe and meaningful way.

How can you foster healthy authenticity at work today?

You long for connection with a deeper purpose and meaning for your life.

You long for connection with yourself.

You long for connection with work.

There is an approach to counseling called gestalt therapy. "Gestalt" is a German word meaning "the whole is greater than the sum of its parts." The goal of gestalt therapy is to help people get in touch with the disconnected parts of themselves and reintegrate them into the whole. Then they can experience life through the most authentic version of themselves.

There is also a biblical model of gestalt: the Triune God. Father, Son, and Holy Spirit, three in one, all connected, one Being with different persons in loving and collaborative union with each other. Genesis 1:26

hints at this: "Then God said, 'Let us make man in *our* image, after *our* likeness'" (italics mine). Jesus also spoke of this oneness in John 10:30: "I and the Father are one."

Healing burnout is not just about figuring out a different work schedule or contemplating a career change. At its root, burnout is the sum of all your disconnected parts. The path to restoration is through oneness, or by a great gestalt. To become whole, you must reconnect your fragmented pieces.

> Burnout is the sum of your disconnected parts.

In the chapters to come, you will become more aware of your disconnection—the threads of your life that have become fragmented. We'll focus on your reconnection to God and the deeper meaning you have from work. Next, we'll focus on developing a deeper awareness of yourself—your personality and experiences that play a role in burnout. Finally, we'll examine the pieces of your work that cause you stress, confusion, or discontentment. You will have the opportunity to do some of the deep soul work I mentioned in chapter 2. It probably won't be easy, but I encourage you to step forward courageously. You can do this!

Light is beginning to break into the grayness of your disconnection. If you open your heart, its warmth will illuminate your landscape into bursts of color. It is the greatest gestalt conceivable.

Chapter 3 Key Points

- Longing is designed to lead you to relationship.
- Authentic connections are the foundation of healthy relationships.
- Burnout is healed through reconnection with God, self, and work.

Practice Being Connected

Be still with God. Remove any distractions that may be present. Sit or lie comfortably, close your eyes, and open your hands. Pray or meditate:

God, everything you do, and everything you want me to do, leads to relationship. Help me remember who you created me to be, and help me live that way authentically. I desire to reconnect with you, with myself, and with my work.

This Week's To-Be List

The Five Intentions of Burnout Resolution

I.
I will practice stillness so God can
restore my soul.

II.
**I will seek connection with God,
myself, and my work.**

III.
I will cultivate awareness of who I am,
where I am, and what I want to be.

IV.
I will take consistent steps to
promote well-being in my work.

V.
I will focus on who I am to *be*,
not what I am to *do*.

4

Be Filled

*I have filled him with the Spirit of God,
with wisdom, with understanding, with
knowledge and all kinds of skills.*

EXODUS 31:3

Steve was a 40-year-old, second-career, burned-out middle school teacher in a Chicago suburb. He loved seeing his students conquer their challenges, but the other aspects of the job, such as dealing with cranky parents and a long commute, eventually took their toll. He managed by shutting down emotionally and pouring himself generous glasses of wine each night. He longed for different work but believed that going back to school at midlife wasn't realistic.

Helping kids was always a passion for Steve. He also valued autonomy and flexibility while helping others at their deepest level of need. This work helped him find meaning in his own life and in his understanding of the world. But now he felt so stuck. He had bills to pay and things to take care of, so he perceived there was no way out.

Steve began searching his soul. What was his true purpose? He was stuck between the desires of his heart and the reasoning of his mind. Things changed for him in a radical aha moment when he realized that being a bit unreasonable is always a component of an exceptional life. The next day, he began searching online for graduate programs in professional counseling.

Are You Hearing Voices?

Steve was experiencing quite a bit of existential angst, otherwise known as a crisis of meaning. Some pieces of his work were meaningful, but other pieces derailed him. As he was considering career number three, he had quite a few questions about his purpose in work, or his vocational calling.

What is a calling? One online dictionary defines it as

1. "the loud cries or shouts of an animal or person" or

2. "a strong urge toward a particular way of life or career; a vocation."[1]

In 1909, Frank Parsons, the founder of a vocational guidance center in Boston (the first in the United States), wrote a book called *Choosing a Vocation*.[2] He wrote this book on the tail end of the industrial revolution. At that time in our nation's history, people didn't feel like work was supposed to be fulfilling. Work was a matter of survival; young adults typically chose the same work their parents did in order to sustain family units. But Parsons believed strongly that work should be about fulfillment and tried to help people find satisfaction in their work.

Parsons believed that career satisfaction came from knowing the self, knowing the world of work, and finding a good fit between the two. This theory makes perfect sense. If you know what you have to offer, and you know the world of work out there, you likely can find a good match. Almost like trying to find your soulmate, right?

But in 1909, this was a new way of thinking, and it shook up the

American workforce. For the first time, workers—which included women and people of color—considered seeking autonomy and self-direction as they developed their careers.

But calling is different from career development. The Latin word for vocation, *vocantem*, means "a call or summons." From the earliest understandings of vocation, work has been equated with calling. There's an implication that calling comes from a deeper place than simply earning a paycheck. It's about finding a greater purpose or deeper meaning in work.

I'm not sure Parsons fully defined the idea of calling, but there are threads of it in his writing. We are hardwired to seek meaning, and one of the most significant ways we pursue it is in our work.

> One of the most significant ways we pursue meaning is in our work.

Why do we equate work with meaning? People need to feel a sense of accomplishment, and productivity and generativity make up a big part of accomplishment. Even if you do not achieve what you set out to do, the pursuit of accomplishment brings you a sense of satisfaction. When you *do* accomplish what you set out to, you also feel satisfied that you contributed to a community or to a greater good.

God created you with the need for achievement and accomplishment, and he gave you the drive for productivity and generativity. He knew that your labor would bring you stress and pain but could also bring you great satisfaction.

Perhaps wrestling through this dissonance is one of the ways in which you find meaning.

Did you choose your vocation? Frank Parsons would have said yes. But let's revisit our definitions of calling. The second definition, "a strong urge toward a particular way of life or career; a vocation," seems plausible. On the surface, the first definition, "loud cries or shouts," doesn't seem to relate to our work. But let's look a little deeper.

A strong urge toward a particular direction likely was present in your career choices. But was something else—something deeper—also present? A voice? You may not have heard this voice audibly, but it was probably there nonetheless. A voice that was leading you to discover the deep meaning through work.

The calling. Your calling.

Rest and Reconnect

Take some time to be still. Reflect on these questions: What is my calling? What does "calling" mean to me?

We'll spend time later on thinking more deeply about your calling. For now, simply become aware of your first response to these questions. Write, doodle, or draw whatever comes to mind.

Calling Received

It's dark, and you are lying in your bed alone. It's a typical Thursday night...wait, now it's an early Friday morning. You haven't gotten any sleep, so in addition to all your other concerns, you'll likely be tired tomorrow at work. You toss and turn and sigh one more time. Anxious thoughts swirl around your brain like water circling a drain. You wonder, *Is my life going down the drain?* (insert anxiety freak-out moment here). You're giving a big presentation tomorrow, and if you don't nail it...well, you're not sure what would happen.

Now imagine the softest, sweetest presence in your room. Hovering over your bed, it's glimmering with light, but it doesn't disturb you. It embraces your forehead and your chest in the most loving way and breathes these words straight into your heart: "It's going to be okay, I've got you." Sleep comes, and you rise with the sun, rested.

What an incredibly comforting and nurturing presence. You couldn't see it, but you experienced it. It gave you peace.

It was the presence of the Holy Spirit.

In Scripture, the Holy Spirit is referred to as breath (Job 33:4), advocate and comforter (John 14:16; 15:26), teacher and helper (John 14:26; 16:13-15), and fire (Acts 2:1-4). In Greek, the masculine pronoun is always used for these images, but the Hebrew word for spirit, *ruach*, is feminine. It refers to breath and life, implying creativity and birth, which have strong feminine and life-giving implications.

The Holy Spirit has a role in how you receive and understand your vocational calling. Consider the story of Ezekiel, a prophet to Israel in the sixth century BC. Ezekiel's calling was to warn the people of the impending destruction of Jerusalem by the Babylonians. Later in his writings, he spoke of hope and God's redemption of the Jews after the desolation.

What a calling! Not many of us can relate to a prophetic calling. But we can relate to God asking us to do something difficult and challenging—maybe even something we don't want to do. It would be so easy to second-guess a calling like this. *Are you sure, God? You're asking me to do what?* How would you know that your calling was really from God and not something you constructed in your mind?

When you are filled with the Holy Spirit, you never have to doubt your calling.

> Like the appearance of a rainbow in the clouds on a rainy day, so was the radiance around him. This was the appearance of the likeness of the glory of the LORD. When I saw it, I fell facedown, and I heard the voice of one speaking. He said to me, "Son of man, stand up on your feet and I will speak to you." As he spoke, the Spirit came into me and raised me to my feet, and I heard him speaking to me (Ezekiel 1:28–2:2).

There was no mistaking that this moment was Ezekiel's calling. What is significant about this story is that God moved toward Ezekiel first. Ezekiel probably didn't even have an awareness of calling until this vision. He definitely didn't ask for such an experience. As I read further in the book of Ezekiel, it sounds like he had a complete freak-out moment!

Women and Men

When I traveled to France many years ago, I was surprised to learn that the most esteemed professions there were not the ones that earned the most money, but those that created the most pleasure. Chocolatiers, sommeliers, and artists are respected and highly valued in France, and only the best succeed.

Not so in the United States. Americans tend to value powerful, high-paying occupations, and those who choose "less ambitious" career paths are often judged less worthy of social esteem. Work often provides a sense of self, validation, and position in communities and families.

For men, this ideal runs deep; they often feel their primary purpose is to be useful and competent. They understand that their drive and work ethic determine their social standing, which affects their self-esteem positively or negatively. For women, this ideal can represent independence and a new sense of accomplishment. It represents a transcendence of the past, and it creates value beyond traditional roles in the home.

To what extent have the vocational ideals of the culture around you shaped your perception of your calling? Think of various expressions of culture, such as your church, your racial and ethnic background, your location, your family values, and any other perspective that has affected you. None of your history has been a mistake; God has a way of using all your experiences, both good and bad, to form your calling. Ask the Holy Spirit to help you understand your calling through your cultural experiences.

There is more to Ezekiel's story. Look at this line: "As he spoke, the Spirit came into me and raised me to my feet." Whether Ezekiel physically stood or this is a metaphor for what he was supposed to do next, there is no mistaking that the Holy Spirit filled him and empowered him to move. It is the same for you. At the point where you meet God, vision or not, the Holy Spirit breathes your calling into your heart.

Have you had an experience like Ezekiel's, when you felt God speaking directly to you, commissioning you to fulfill your calling? I've known some people who have, but I've known more people who haven't. Instead, they've described it as a knowing or an intuition—a still, small voice.

Calling is realized through stillness, when the mind quiets and the heart opens. The Holy Spirit moves toward you; your heart receives and experiences fullness once again.

A Matter of the Heart

Okay, Amy—great info, but this whole calling thing isn't news to me. I even think I know what my calling is. Why does it matter?

Because calling is where all this began for you. You've known your whole life that you would have a job or a career. You even chose the job or career you're in right now, and you might have wrestled with career decisions for many years. I'll bet that you've even spent a lot of time training for your career. But along the way, did you have a conscious awareness that God designed you in a unique way for a unique purpose that only you could fulfill?

Earlier in the chapter, I asked you to think about your calling. Take a few moments to let that answer crystallize in your mind. In your state of burnout, it could be hard to answer that question. You might know what your calling used to be, but perhaps you've lost fervor for it. Perhaps you never knew what it was, so you began your career open to wherever you ended up.

It's that sense of lost calling that has gotten you stuck. You know you are called. You have moved within that calling, and for a while, you felt fulfillment and meaning from the work it led you to. But now you can't *feel* it, and that makes you question everything. The dissonance between knowing and feeling results in existential angst.

It's a crisis that's hard to name because your mind doesn't understand it. You are working in a job you thought you would love. A job that once was fulfilling. Everything adds up on paper: You trained for this work because it was something you thought you would enjoy. You climbed the career ladder because you were good at your job. You stayed because you could see results. So why do you feel so empty?

Emptiness comes from the heart, not from the mind.

> Perhaps being a bit unreasonable is always a component of an exceptional life.

Steve knew that emptiness all too well. In his mind, he tried to explain it away, to rationalize why he was feeling the way he was. It wasn't until he accepted that his purpose—his calling—came from a different place than his mind that he was open to taking the next step. When he was able to move out of his mind and into his heart, he moved.

Calling is unreasonable in the sense that it isn't rational. It doesn't come from the mind. It comes from the heart, breathed there softly, passionately by the Holy Spirit.

The Holy Spirit often commissions you to do things that are not rational. But it is always for a greater purpose—both yours and others. It is by stepping into that purpose that you find meaning. Consider Exodus 31:3: "I have filled him with the Spirit of God, with wisdom, with understanding, with knowledge and with all kinds of skills." The Holy Spirit is directly linked to how you manifest meaning in your work.

You are empty, friend. Your heart is longing to be filled. You've called this emptiness "burnout," but my guess is that it's much deeper than burnout. The good news? The Holy Spirit is all about filling empty hearts. In fact, that's his whole purpose. To fill you. To refresh you.

To revive your energy—for work, for life, and for your quest toward deeper meaning.

Reconnect with the Holy Spirit, and you will be filled—emptiness and existential angst and spiritual vocation crisis and all. It starts with your heart first because that's where you find joy and meaning in work. Your true calling, found.

Rest and Reconnect

Have you ever heard the phrase "Father, Son, and Holy Spirit" and wondered why they are placed in that order? God the Father often is equated with the mind, Jesus with the body, and the Holy Spirit with the heart. In this way, it's easy to conceptualize the mind-and-body part of working; our work is often governed by executive functioning and physical labor. But how might your thinking change about your work if you reordered them? The Holy Spirit moves toward you and places vocational calling in your heart. How might your view of work change if you started there?

Chapter 4 Key Points

- Calling is connected to your sense of meaning.
- The Holy Spirit breathes calling into your heart.
- Be filled with the Holy Spirit, who refreshes your energy for work.

Practice Being Filled

Be still with the Holy Spirit. Remove any distractions that may be present. Sit or lie comfortably, close your eyes, and open your hands. Pray or meditate:

Holy Spirit, I open my heart to your presence. Fill me. Reveal to me the calling you have placed in my heart.

Write, doodle, or draw what the Holy Spirit shows you. If you are struggling with understanding your calling or are feeling chronically empty about work, I encourage you to practice this on a regular basis. It may take some time for the Holy Spirit to reveal your calling, as he tends to work through people and circumstances as well as his presence. But rest assured, if you do this practice regularly, the Holy Spirit will be faithful to fill you and reveal truth to you.

Your calling provides direction to follow in your work life, but it can change over time. Your passions and interests can become more or less fine-tuned, which is a natural result of growth. Sometimes God has new assignments for you. We'll revisit this idea again in chapter 14.

This Week's To-Be List

_____

_____

_____

_____

_____

_____

_____

_____

_____

_____

_____

_____

_____

_____

_____

_____

_____

_____

5

Be Nourished

Then Jesus declared, "I am the bread of life.
Whoever comes to me will never go hungry, and
whoever believes in me will never be thirsty."

JOHN 6:35

You can probably guess from the title what this chapter is about. You might be rolling your eyes or even bracing yourself for a lecture on the importance of taking care of your health. Yeah, I might give you a bit of a lecture, but it'll be just a tiny one. And what I have learned about your physical health and burnout might surprise you.

Let's start with this: Dear Friend, I completely understand how frustrated you are with your body right now.

I understand your frustration because I've been there. I've lived through years of chronic stress from work, and I know what it's like to try to function in my body while it's falling apart in front of my eyes. I know what it's like to have insomnia, to gain unwanted weight, and to suffer from an autoimmune disorder. Forever, I denied that my physical health conditions were related to stress. I just tried to pull myself up by my bootstraps and get back to work.

But here's an undeniable, research-supported fact: Stress wreaks havoc on your physical body, and eventually your body begins to protest and give way. In fact, one of the first indicators of chronic stress and burnout is the development of physical health problems. It's easy to go and go and go...until your body won't go anymore. In that moment of crisis, you begin to realize, *Okay, this burnout thing is serious...I need to do something about it.*

> One of the first indicators of chronic stress and burnout is the development of physical health problems.

While burnout can affect any area of your physical health, the most prevalent areas are sleep, weight gain, and the development of chronic health problems.[1] A lack of sleep affects your mental sharpness, and job stress has been associated with weight gain.[2] These contribute to longer-term health problems, such as mental health issues, IBS, autoimmune disorders, and other chronic conditions.[3] These issues can motivate you to take care of your burnout!

It didn't work out very well for me to deny the connection between my work stress and the deterioration of my physical health. So here's my (tiny) lecture: You need to take care of your physical health. Otherwise, you will eventually become incapacitated and not be able to work anymore. End of lecture.

It's easier to take care of your physical health than you might think. If you feel unhappy with your body's current functioning, there is great hope. I'll share a few insights that helped me, and then I'll let you do some research on your own. There's enough body-health shaming these days, and you don't need any more from me. You are smart. I trust you will take what you need from this chapter and use it to your fullest advantage.

Jesus Gets It

Jesus understands the limitations of our physical bodies. As God incarnate, Jesus experienced all the bodily functions that humans do. Like...diarrhea. Vomiting. Disgust from unpleasant smells. Food preferences. He probably even experienced penile erections—he was a man, after all.

I just heard a collective gasp from all my conservative readers! If I offended you by that last statement, please remember who designed our bodies. Nothing is wrong with how we physically function, including how we sexually function.

We also know that Jesus experienced extreme fatigue. As I read the Gospels, I see signs of burnout during his ministry. But Scripture also shows that he took care of his physical health. For example, in Matthew 14, we see that he rested and ate. He moved his body. And he interacted with his community.

Jesus gets your frustration with your physical body. And he also provided a model to take care of yourself.

It's so easy to deny the needs of our physical bodies. It's so easy to overschedule each day so there's no time to exercise. It's so easy to eat and drink too much during office lunches. It's so easy to work "just a couple more hours" after the kids go to bed. But your body is now screaming that these habits are not going to work for you in the long run.

If Jesus—the omnipotent, omniscient, and omnipresent God of the universe—took care of his physical body, you can too.

Bio-What?

This year, I experienced a radical change in my physical health. In my midforties, I felt as if my body was a runaway train headed for a cliff with no bridge. I knew that if I didn't do something different, I would crash and burn. I had been struggling with asthma for years, which kept worsening despite all the dietary and lifestyle changes I tried. Using a steroid inhaler twice a day was not a sustainable plan. So I got the name of a naturopath and made an appointment.

We met together a few times, and she ran some tests. On the day of the test results, she walked in with a three-page printout and a compassionate smile.

"You have a food intolerance, and it's a hard one," she said.

Oh no. Was it gluten? Dairy? I couldn't imagine life without cheese and chocolate. Having a Trader Joe's peanut butter cup is sometimes the only thing that gets me through a stressful afternoon.

"It's fruit," she said simply.

Fruit? Like apples and blueberries and bananas? Fruit that I had eaten every day since I was a kid, good-for-you fruit, "mom taught me to eat it instead of eating candy" fruit?

Yep. It was fruit.

I couldn't believe it. "Are you sure?" I asked. How could I have an intolerance to an entire food group, let alone a natural, unprocessed, nutrient-filled thing God made?

And then she said something that transformed the way I think about nutrition and physical health. "Do you have ancestry from Northern Europe? Patients with this intolerance tend to have bloodlines from that part of the world. People there don't eat fruit because they don't need it. It doesn't grow there."

I immediately ordered a genetic test and confirmed that most of my ancestry is from Northern and Eastern Europe. My naturopath had informed me about bio-individuality, which means your physical needs are determined by your genetics.

There is not a one-size-fits-all approach to physical health, which means that any diet or any book that promotes a health and nutrition solution may or may not be true for you. It all depends on your genetics or personal biology. Therefore, it's unrealistic for me to provide a comprehensive guide addressing physical health and burnout for you. Instead, let's focus on general concepts of self-care from Jesus's example: rest, nutrition, movement, and touch.

Rest

Rest. Doesn't it sound like a wonderful word? Even luxurious? But rest should *never* be considered a luxury. It's a *necessity*. In fact, it's the very first thing that needs to happen to heal your burnout.

Rest is the first part of the word "restore." It means that you restore energy to your body, mind, and soul. It is not exactly the same thing as sleep, although sleep is a big part of rest. When you are in a state of burnout, you are depleted. The very first step to healing is to be *rest*ored.

When was the last time you felt truly rested? Think about it for a minute. Really, think about it. Was it before your current job—or maybe before you had children? How about in college? (Nah, no one feels rested in college!) How about when you were a kid?

Has it really been that long since you've felt rested?

If your life is like mine, you are up and on every day. The problem is, sometimes you never turn it off. And then your body gets hijacked and won't turn off, even if you want it to. That's called adrenal fatigue. The stress hormones adrenaline, cortisol, and norepinephrine become dysregulated. In this state, you will have a hard time sleeping. You may experience fatigue at points in the day when you don't want to, so you reach for stimulants (coffee and donuts) to give you the boost you need to get through. You may feel chronically tired, which also makes you feel chronically irritable, depressed, anxious...and a slew of other physical and mental symptoms.

Here are a few suggestions for rest:

Practice good sleep hygiene. Figure out how many hours of sleep your body needs to function at its best. Use that information to create a schedule for going to bed and rising, and follow that schedule every day. Turn off blue screens an hour or two before bed, and opt instead to read, stretch, or make love with your sweetie before going to sleep.

Take a nap during your workday. Yes, you read that correctly. When you feel a pull toward sugar or coffee, especially in the afternoon, your body is telling you that it is *tired*, not hungry. Drink a glass of water and then lay down for a nap. Don't worry—you won't sleep all afternoon!

Your bladder will wake you 20 or 30 minutes later. I keep a yoga mat, a blanket, and two pillows in my office, and a nap makes all the difference in my ability to finish my workday productively and be present during my evening activities. If your boss looks at you cross-eyed when she learns you are sleeping in your office, tell her that a 20-minute nap can improve attention and cognitive processing.

Practice a weekly Sabbath. God designed a Sabbath specifically for rest; he himself rested (Genesis 2:2). One day each week, commit to not doing any work. Instead, focus on doing things that reconnect you to God, yourself, and others.

Intentionally do things that restore your soul. Participate in activities that restore you instead of those that deplete your energy. For example, if you are a parent, you might opt to spend a quiet night cooking and eating dinner with your kids at seven o'clock instead of attending their noisy basketball game at five and grabbing Taco Bell afterward because you are too exhausted to do anything else. Let their other parent take them to the game, and then enjoy a pleasant, healthy dinner together later. (Yes, this is okay!)

If your body has reached a state of chronic unrest—adrenal fatigue—it's time for a radical intervention. Please go see your doctor or naturopath, read up on adrenal fatigue, and get a plan in place to heal your body. If you don't, the physical consequences could be grave.

Nutrition

When you are burned out, you need to eat more food.

You probably didn't see that one coming. In fact, I'll guess that you have been eating more food lately. Perhaps you are craving certain foods, or you have weird meal schedules because of work travel. Perhaps you are struggling with binge eating to curb your anxiety, or even skipping meals because of an upset stomach or loss of appetite. Whatever the case, your body needs adequate nutrition and water in order to function at its best. So do eat more food, but make sure the food you eat is full of nutrients.

Please note that I did not title this section "diet." I've heard that word enough in my life, and I'm guessing you have too. We are inundated with diet information every day. We are surrounded by images of perfect bodies alongside grandiose images of food, but the theme running through it all is deprivation.

It's human nature to immediately want to correct deprivation by hoarding or by making sure we get more than we need. It's part of the survival nature. And when you hear a deprivation term like "diet," it sets off a panic within the brain. For example, when you start the newest fad diet and you can't eat pizza, you suddenly crave pizza, right? *I won't eat pizza, I won't eat pizza*...and then you eat pizza. And then you probably overdo it because your brain is laser-focused on that pizza from a place of deprivation.

Remember, when you are burned out, you are experiencing depletion. A diet isn't going to work. Can you approach your nutrition from a place of fullness? Instead of taking away things that you deem bad, focus on adding more of the good stuff.

Instead of *no more pizza*, add enough vegetables to fill half your plate.

Instead of *I'm cutting out coffee*, add 32 ounces of water the first thing in the morning.

Instead of *no more eating out*, add three home-cooked, healthy meals a week.

When you add good things, your body will respond in good ways. I guarantee it.

To heal, you must restore. This is exactly why a deprivation diet model will not work. It will only further break down your body. Bio-individuality determines what you should or should not eat, not the latest and greatest, lose-12-pounds-this-weekend fad diet. I encourage you to visit a naturopath, nutritionist, or health coach to design a plan just for you. Focus on restoring nutrients that have been depleted by chronic stress.

> Focus on *rest* and *increasing nutrition* rather than a strict diet and exercise plan.

Rest and Reconnect

With all the health misinformation available, it's easy to approach wellness and health care from an attitude of deprivation or shame. This attitude creates an unhealthier cycle in the long run. A more realistic approach is the cultivation of health, which is achieved by small, daily habits. What is one new habit you can start tomorrow that will cultivate your health? What is one habit you can stop tomorrow that will improve your health?

Movement

Again, did you notice that I didn't use the word "exercise"? You already know you need to exercise. But when you are burned out, strenuous exercise can actually make it worse. You might be telling yourself, *I have to get to the gym every day after work,* because you don't like the extra curvature that now rounds off your middle. News flash: This behavior is not going to work out well in the long run. Please remember that your body is depleted. Whatever you do should replace your energy instead of taking it away. Vigorous and strenuous exercise activates your stress hormones just as much as a heated conversation with your boss.

It's easy to get caught up in thinking you have to exercise. I would invite you to consider finding something you *want* to do, at least for a while. Set a goal for movement instead of exercise. Start simple: Move enough to sweat 20 minutes a day—that's it. If you can't muster going to the gym to get sweaty, then give yourself a break and try hot yoga or sit in a sauna.

What kind of exercise restores you? Identify a few and try those instead. Perhaps a walk with your sweetie after work, chasing your kids on their skateboards at the park, yoga, or hiking outdoors. Bonus points if you can integrate other forms of physical wellness, like touch. Which brings us to the next point...

Touch

I don't often see touch mentioned in wellness plans. But oh, touch needs to be part of your physical wellness. Touch is important in bonding, giving and receiving affection, and feeling loved. When safe and wanted, touch lowers blood pressure and anxiety and increases overall feelings of well-being.

When I was talking about rest, did you notice that I suggested that you "make love with your sweetie before going to sleep"? Sexual activity is a wonderful healing agent for burnout. Skin-to-skin contact increases the hormone oxytocin, the human bonding hormone. Orgasm releases endorphins to the brain, which reduce anxiety and depression and boost your ability to focus. Orgasm also helps you sleep better. Sex is a double whammy because it helps you get both rest and touch. So go tell your sweetie that you need to have more sex to heal your burnout. Doctor's orders!

If sex isn't an option for you right now, consider activities where you can enjoy safe and loving touch, such as regular massages, hugs from loved ones, or playing with pets. Contact sports, such as basketball or football or wrestling with your kids, are other means of touch that can feel less emotionally overwhelming while releasing a lot of tension.

Each of these areas is important alone, but they also work together. If you start with rest, you think more clearly and can make better decisions about nutrition. When you are getting the proper amount of nutrients and water, you have more energy to move. When you move regularly, you feel better about your body and more open to giving and receiving touch. And then your rest improves. And so on...

One healthy choice can lead to the next healthy choice. Little by little, you cultivate physical wellness.

In case you are wondering, my health improved amazingly since eliminating fruit. It did require some major dietary changes on my part, which was hard—but it paid off. I had to give up wine and marionberry pie forever, but when I removed the trigger of inflammation, my asthma completely disappeared. Since I am now able to move without wheezing, I started running again, and I lost 25 pounds without out even trying. My sleep regulated with exercise, especially because I work out at the same time every morning. My brain fog cleared, my mood improved, and everything just got generally better. And I still eat peanut butter cups!

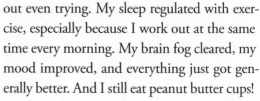

Discover what your unique body needs to function at its best.

Please don't think that eliminating fruit will do the same thing for you. It may or may not. Instead, discover your bio-individuality. Work to find what your unique body needs to function at its best. Develop your physical wellness plan for rest, nutrition, movement, and touch, and write it into your day planner before you even begin to schedule your work commitments.

And then do that.

Communion

If you grew up in the church as I did, you are probably well aware of the lack of information or emphasis on caring for your physical body. In fact, at the last church potluck I attended, the healthiest thing available was "organic" potato chips!

I love that the Scripture includes stories of Jesus attending to his physical needs. Even though Jesus is God, he experienced all the physical limitations of humans. His example of care for the physical body should extend into our church teaching, our homes, and our own lives.

You cannot achieve your work goals if your body is broken down. Care for the body should come first before you do any mind tasks. After all, the body houses the mind. Without proper nutrition, digestion, rest, movement, and touch, our brains do not function at their best. And then you do not function at your best.

As Christians, we participate in the ceremony of communion

(Matthew 26:26-28), which is not only a remembrance of the death and resurrection of Jesus but also an act of oneness with God. Receiving food and drink into your physical body is a tangible symbol of receiving Jesus into your being. From this oneness, you are made whole; you are nourished. In the immanence of communion, care of your physical body becomes a sacred act.

Ask Jesus to teach you about your unique physical needs. Spend some time in oneness with him, meditating on the fact that he also experienced a physical body. He created your body, and he will show you exactly what you need to take care of it. He will lead you to the correct information. He will help you find the right people to help you—coaches, naturopaths, doctors, and supportive friends. He will encourage you when you feel discouraged.

May you be nourished.

Chapter 5 Key Points

- Jesus understands your physical limitations.
- Take care of your physical body through rest, nutrition, movement, and touch.
- Connect with Jesus through the practice of communion.

Practice Being Nourished

Be still with Jesus. Remove any distractions that may be present. Sit or lie comfortably, close your eyes, and open your hands. Pray or meditate:

Jesus, I find communion with you in this moment. Help me understand you, and help me find comfort in your understanding of me. Teach me what I need to know to take care of my physical body.

Write, doodle, or draw what Jesus teaches you.

This Week's To-Be List

6

Be Accepted

*We have seen his glory, the glory of the
one and only Son, who came from the
Father, full of grace and truth.*

JOHN 1:14

felt like I was wrapped in a damp electric blanket. Muggy and
oppressive, the heat never relented, even during the long nights that
buzzed and hummed with strange sounds. The stench—burning
trash, raw sewage, and the swamp cabbage growing outside my bug
hut—turned my stomach continually. I didn't know if I was suffering
from a bacterial infection or spiritual or psychological unease.

I was in Banda Aceh, Indonesia, in July 2005. Seven months after
the Indian Ocean tsunami, I deployed there to assist with mental
health disaster relief. My job was to help survivors process their loss.

Their losses were indescribable. Mothers survived alone after their
babies were pulled out of their hands. Villages were completely washed
away by the unmerciful waves. Homes, families, and entire communities were crushed to bits.

I knew the trip was going to be hard, but I was determined to go. This was the mission of Jesus to a broken world, and I could do it. Packing my bags, it seemed almost selfish to think of my own needs for the journey. The people whose lives had been devastated by the tsunami were my only priority. My needs were inconsequential.

But within days, my stomach became sick and my heart became even sicker. How could a good God allow something like this to happen? I surely didn't have any explanation for it. My whole spiritual framework was being rocked to its core. The only thing that consoled me was a tube of cucumber foot lotion that I had tossed into my suitcase. Actually, I had packed it to appease my mother, who sent it to me specifically for the trip. It was extra weight in an already bulging suitcase, but Mama always knows best, right?

She was right. I learned more from that tube of cucumber lotion than I ever dreamed.

A Good Daddy

In chapter 5, we considered the importance of taking care of our physical bodies. While I tried to be kind, I was still firm. As Christians, we're familiar with a stern approach, aren't we? It's what we expect from Christian culture. If we're not mindful about this, we can begin viewing God as an authoritarian figure, disinterested and removed from our lives, just waiting to drop the hatchet or to say "I told you so" when something goes wrong.

For me, connection with Father has always been the hardest. As mentioned, I grew up in a conservative church. I learned to interpret Scripture literally, and there was no wiggle room for things like nose piercings, man buns, or dancing. As a result, I developed a distorted view of Father—a distant, unemotional, masculine figure who was always disappointed in me.

I'm not quite sure how I developed this view. My own father was very kind, as were most of the Christian men around me. It took years of searching Scripture (particularly, understanding the message of redemption in the books of the prophets), prayer, and the pain of my own life journey to reconceptualize my view of Father.

I think many Christians view Father the way I used to. And this view can be very, very difficult if you are experiencing burnout. Lack of connection with Father can leave you feeling as if the rug has been pulled out from under your feet. It's a feeling of being lost, unsafe, and unseen—a wanderer with no home. Yet at the same time, you fear going back home because you know you will be asked to face the truth.

It's such a precarious juxtaposition; a desire to run straight into your Daddy's arms while running as fast and as far away from him as you can get.

Friend, I am going to say this next statement as lovingly and as gently as possible: There are truths you must face about your burnout. There are things deep inside you that got you to this place of exhaustion. There are things about your work environment that got you here. These truths will likely be hard to face, but without facing them, you will not heal.

> **There are truths to face about your burnout.**

If the last thing you want right now is more hard stuff, I understand. So before we dive into it, let me help you reconceptualize your view of Father. As a strong, protective Daddy, he wants nothing more than for you to heal, to find peace, and to live your best possible life. He wants you to run straight into his arms so he can lift you above your circumstances, spin you around in delight, and gently set you down in a spacious place.

I'm going to show you the Father's truth so you can embrace him as he lovingly reveals to you the truth of your life. But I'm not going to start with religion. I'm going to start with psychotherapy.

Is Your Thinking Burning You Out?

One of the most popular counseling approaches today is called cognitive behavioral therapy (CBT). The premise of CBT is that sometimes we have unhelpful ways of thinking, and those patterns get us stuck. If we can change the way we think, then we will change the way we feel and behave. In CBT, clients become aware of their thoughts and then are challenged by the therapist to change them into healthier ways of thinking,

The trickiest thinking patterns are the shoulds, have-tos, and musts.

I *should* be on time.

I *have to* do everything perfectly.

I *must* sign this sales deal.

Have you ever struggled with should, have-to, or must thinking? It can create a lot of anxiety. It's usually learned from values that form early in life. These thoughts become automatic; as we grow, we don't really stop to critically think about our values and how they are serving us—or not. Values are great things. But as adults, we are responsible for consciously choosing our values and living them out authentically. Otherwise, we are living someone else's life.

Shoulds, have-tos, and musts trigger deep fear in my heart. *I'm not good enough. I won't make it. I don't have what it takes. I'm such a disappointment.* (That last one is the worst.)

Christians have another layer of rules and conformity norms. Consider this story from Luke 7:36-39:

> When one of the Pharisees invited Jesus to have dinner with him, he went to the Pharisee's house and reclined at the table. A woman in that town who lived a sinful life learned that Jesus was eating at the Pharisee's house, so she came there with an alabaster jar of perfume. As she stood behind him at his feet weeping, she began to wet his feet with her tears. Then she wiped them with her hair, kissed them, and poured perfume on them. When the Pharisee who had invited him saw this, he said to himself, "If this man were a prophet, he would know who is touching him and what kind of woman she is— that she is a sinner."

This story reveals a clear cultural and religious expectation for appropriate behavior.

The woman "who had lived a sinful life" was not only wasting a valuable resource but also touching a man in a public display of emotion. Onlookers likely assumed she had obtained the perfume through dubious means. In a culture that was predominantly poor and patriarchal, these behaviors would have been deemed disgusting.

But Jesus wasn't about the rules. He saw the larger context of the situation; he saw her heart.

> Do you see this woman? I came to your house. You did not give me any water for my feet, but she wet my feet with her tears and wiped them with her hair. You did not give me a kiss, but this woman, from the time I entered, has not stopped kissing my feet. You did not put oil on my head, but she has poured perfume on my feet. Therefore, I tell you, her many sins have been forgiven—as her great love has shown. But whoever has been forgiven little loves little (Luke 7:44-47).

Jesus sees past the shoulds, have-tos, and musts—straight to the heart. With Jesus, it's always about love, because love is the foundation of grace.

You probably feel pressure to perform and produce at work. Rules and standards do serve a purpose. They help you grow, and they help you work toward excellence. They also keep order, which is important in the workplace. But when your thinking is so rule-based that there's no room for love, you'll naturally be stressed out, afraid, and disappointed.

Love is the foundation of grace.

How have automatic thoughts shown up in your work/career? Are they working for you or not working for you? Take a moment and reflect on this question. Better yet, this week at work, try to become aware of how the shoulds, have-tos, and musts are showing up.

I'd like to invite you to consider a different way.

Rest and Reconnect

In CBT, people learn to change their unhelpful thinking patterns (including shoulds, have-tos, and musts) into more helpful ones. This process requires you to become aware of your automatic thoughts and consciously change them to empowering thoughts. For example, if you automatically think, *I should be on time*, how might your perspective change if you thought, *I choose to be on time*?

Try it! For the rest of the day, become aware of any thoughts that automatically conform to rules or old values. Consciously try to change those thoughts or language to *I choose to* or *I want to* or *I will* or *It is important to me to...* Note whether this one small step changes your perspective.

Grace Changes Everything

Do you remember Mitchell from chapter 1? His life was quickly descending into chaos. I'll bet you can relate. As you will learn in the following chapters, those of us who are high performers, who care deeply about work, or who are givers tend to experience burnout more than others. It's a powerless, exhausting feeling. And then we feel like such big disappointments.

There is grace for you.

Grace is such a big part of Christian shoptalk, we often miss its counterintuitive, mind-boggling meaning. In workplace environments managed by employee handbooks (rules), it's hard to imagine how grace even fits in our day-to-day lives. So I'd like to offer this definition: Grace means that when you have come to the end of yourself, you are still enough.

It means that when you are in your office with the door locked, trying to practice deep breathing because you are so overwhelmed, you are enough.

It means that when you have locked yourself in the bathroom stall at work, crying out, *God, I cannot do this work. I cannot be in this environment. It is impossible for me to do this one more second. I don't want to. I can't...*in that desperate moment, you are enough.

It means that when you are angry or frustrated with having the same conversation with your work colleagues and you lose your temper, you are still enough.

It means that when you have come to the end of yourself, when you are out of resources, when you are out of energy, Father whispers, *Beloved, I have never loved you more than I do in this moment. You are always enough because my grace covers everything you cannot.*

It makes you rethink your expectations for yourself, doesn't it? You never were expected to be enough. All you ever needed to do was to show up, because everything else is already covered. When you accept grace, you always live in the fullest version of yourself. Because you have experienced the pain of being broken, you are humble. But because of Father's lavish grace, you are whole and empowered.

You might be beating yourself up right now, especially if things have fallen apart. The shoulds, have-tos, and musts might be running rampant through your brain, triggering your failure fears. Does this mean you stop trying? Not at all (Romans 6:15). Instead, it means that when you've come to the end of yourself, you can let go and accept grace. And in your acceptance of God's grace, you realize what acceptance really means—perhaps for the very first time. You are worthy, lovable, and desired *just as you are*.

It's not an accident that John 1:14 mentions grace first and then truth. God moves toward you first with grace because you can't hear the truth until you experience God's grace—his deep, transformative, transcendent, all-consuming love. If you heard truth first, you would just shut down and become even more alienated. Exactly the opposite of what God wants in your relationship with him and others.

Grace. A gift that changes everything when we accept and receive it. Especially our burnout.

Women and Men

How do women and men perceive grace in the workplace? As employees or workers, grace isn't really something we think about. You have a job description, you try to get the job done, you get a paycheck, and you have a performance review to determine whether you'll get a raise or be fired. This seems much more like an environment based on rules and order than on grace. How might your workplace change if you could adopt the motto, "I am enough, and you are enough"? I challenge you to write this statement and put it on a Post-it note near your computer or phone—somewhere you will see it often. Better yet, put it on the mirror in the bathroom, and observe how your work environment could change!

Father Doesn't Do Performance Reviews

I experienced one of my deepest seasons of burnout during my month in Indonesia. I was tired before I left; the 36-hour journey was the first downtime I'd had since finishing my PhD. The ensuing culture shock and exposure to vast, devastating trauma completely did me in. It was hard for me to face my assignment, and for the first time in my career, I felt that I wasn't going to be able to finish something I started. Facing that fact provoked deep questions and spiritual unrest in my heart. All I wanted was to get on the next plane home.

I felt like such a failure.

Most of the Indonesian survivors' stories were lost through miscommunication with the translator. I couldn't understand their words, and most of the time I couldn't understand the cultural nuances. But I could understand their eyes and voices. Most days, all I could manage was a smile, an appropriate touch, and sitting with them as they cried. By the grace of God, it was enough.

So I continued to show up—to get out of my bug hut every morning, sweaty before I even got to the bath. I walked every day. The brand-new sandals I had purchased for the trip rubbed against my feet, smearing blood over the cracked, dirty calluses on my heels.

Removing my sandals each evening signaled relief that the day was over. I had made it through one more day, and I could rest. I could not bear to get into my bed with dirty feet, so I washed them every night and rubbed them with the cucumber lotion that my mother insisted I take with me. She could see the journey ahead of me, and she knew I would need it. Washing my feet and rubbing them helped me feel grounded. The scent reminded me of home and my mother, and I felt comforted. It was a way to connect with what I knew while trying to survive a foreign and scary place.

In the midst of abject poverty and feeling the poverty of my own heart and spirit, I lavished cucumber lotion on my feet as Father lavished his grace on me.

Grace is the wisdom of Father to see your stress and pain even before it arrives. To provide a way through it even with small things that you would not even dream could bring you comfort. To connect you with your sense of home. To make you feel normal when everything is a disaster. To give you something to look forward to when you have come to the end of yourself.

He wants to lavish his grace on you and in you. This is Abba Father, Daddy, your strong Papa. He's not your authoritarian boss. He's not your malicious coworker. He's not pointing out all your flaws or doing a performance review.

He's home, waiting to greet you at the end of your long workday.

He wants you there with him, just as you are, smelly feet and all. No shoulds, have-tos, or musts. Just you in your perfectly imperfect, exhausted state. Acceptance *is* receiving. Reach up your arms to him and let him lavish his affection on you.

Chapter 6 Key Points

- God moves toward you in grace and truth.
- Grace comes first so that you can hear God's truth.
- In your burnout, Father lavishes his grace on you.

Practice Receiving God's Lavish Grace

Be still with Father God. Remove any distractions that may be present. Sit or lie comfortably, close your eyes, and open your hands. Pray or meditate:

Father, I open my heart to receive your grace. I open my mind to receive your truth. Reveal to me what I need to know about my burnout. Restore me. I choose to trust you.

The next three chapters transition to the third intention of burnout resolution. These chapters might be a little hard because they talk about personal things that may have gotten you to your burnout state. As you read them, give yourself grace and withhold judgment. That's the spirit in which I wrote them. If you ever feel overwhelmed, turn back to chapters 4 through 6 and spend time reconnecting with God. He's there to support you through the hard stuff. I'm here with you too!

This Week's To-Be List

_____

_____

_____

_____

_____

_____

_____

_____

_____

_____

_____

_____

_____

_____

_____

_____

The Five Intentions of Burnout Resolution

I.
I will practice stillness so God can
restore my soul.

II.
I will seek connection with God,
myself, and my work.

III.
I will cultivate awareness of who I am,
where I am, and what I want to be.

IV.
I will take consistent steps to
promote well-being in my work.

V.
I will focus on who I am to *be*,
not what I am to *do*.

7

Be Free

It is for freedom that Christ has set us free.

GALATIANS 5:1

Your phone is blowing up, and you know exactly what that means. It's an emergency. As a bona fide first responder, this is your shtick. Something shifts in your brain, and you go into "the zone." Your half-finished breakfast no longer matters. Your raging adrenaline feeds all your physical needs. You grab your phone and your go bag—your bag of supplies that are always packed for situations like this—and you head out the door to the scene.

Superhero to the Rescue

Does this situation sound familiar? You may be an EMT or paramedic, emergency room medical professional, member of the military, fire professional, or police officer. More likely, you don't work in any of those professions—but you operate as a first responder anyway.

Of course, I'm talking about the need to rescue others—to help them with whatever they need, whenever they call. It's a noble quality, really. They are helped, and you enjoy the satisfaction of helping. I'm not criticizing the desire to help. But unchecked, it can create a whole lot of burnout.

Herbert Freudenberger, one of the first researchers of burnout, believed that unfulfilled expectations are at the root of burnout. You begin work or your career with wishes unknown to your conscious mind, which quickly develop into a template of behavioral expectations for yourself and others. Of course, this template doesn't work out too well because others don't always behave the way you expect them to. In fact, sometimes you don't behave the way you expect yourself to!

Freudenberger believed the dissonance between what is expected or wished for, and what is real, is the ultimate root of burnout.

In chapter 6, you learned about automatic thoughts—especially the shoulds, have-tos, and musts—which are developed from values you are taught early in life. Another type of automatic thought is *I need, or else...*

I need refers to something you desire or do to calm a deep fear (*or else*). The fear is connected to your core wounds, which come from painful experiences and shape your deepest needs. You feel a very strong pull, or drive, to meet the *I need* even though you might not be able to consciously identify it in the moment. In fact, you experience psychological tension until that need is met, which creates all kinds of *interesting* behavior.

Here are a few examples of how the *I need, or else* drive manifests in the psyche:

"*I need* to be touched, *or else* I am unlovable."

"*I need* to be in charge, *or else* I will lose control."

"*I need* to rescue others from their pain, *or else* I won't matter to them."

I used the language "manifests on the psyche" intentionally. Since this drive comes from such a deep place, you may never have awareness of it. It's easier to recognize maladaptive thoughts than it is to become aware of unconscious needs. Since your unconscious needs are connected to your deepest pain, becoming aware of them is usually extremely difficult. It's not a fun process to sit with your pain, feel it, and learn to let it go.

For example, let's say you grew up with an alcoholic parent. You spent many lonely nights as a child, wondering if your parent was going to get home in one piece and if anyone was going to take care of you. Fast-forward 20 years, when you become a basketball coach at a rural high school. Your students have challenges; many of them also have parents struggling with acute substance abuse. Each day, you spend a few hours after practice going above and beyond your coach duties...because you care and because you want to make sure that your team will be successful.

An exemplary work ethic? A kindhearted, competent professional? Absolutely. But look a little deeper. What if your unconscious motivation was, "*I need* to take care of these kids, *or else* no one else will"? Or, "*I need* to be the best coach ever, *or else* no one will like me"? You are doing a great job and meeting your students' needs, but you are also striving to meet an unmet need within yourself.

Now, I want to be very clear that it's okay for you to have needs. It's okay for you to strive to meet them. It's okay to work hard and to help people. What gets you into trouble is being *unaware* of your needs. If you aren't aware of what is driving you to work the way you do, and if your work doesn't fulfill those unconscious needs, you burn out.

Let's loop back to the need to rescue, or the superhero mentality. I'm dedicating an entire chapter to this because unconscious needs contribute the most to burnout. The need to help others, or to take their pain away, is one of the deepest desires of the human heart. It is beautiful because it comes from a place of empathy and relationship; God designed you with the desire to love, care for, and connect with others. However, when it becomes more about you than them, it wreaks havoc on your entire being, creating more distress for those around you in the long run.

Rest and Reconnect

What unmet expectations might be contributing to your burnout?

All of us begin our jobs or careers with expectations; few of us are aware of those expectations. Spend a few minutes reflecting on what you wished for in your current job or career. For example, you may have desired to use your creative skills but feel frustrated when you are stopped by bureaucratic systems. Or you may have hoped to have a team spirit with your coworkers and are frustrated by their attitudes.

What you wish for turns into expectations for yourself and for others. What frustrates you the most at work? This could be a clue about your unconscious expectations or needs.

Take a few moments to journal, doodle, or draw. We'll revisit these questions later in the chapter.

Only One Superhero

Christians are often more susceptible to the superhero mentality than secular people. Why? We pick it up from the Christian culture. Jesus gave everything—literally his life—which becomes the unspoken expectation in the church. *Keep sacrificing, keep giving as much as you can, just like Jesus would.* But is sacrificing to the point of death—even an emotional death—really what Jesus asked us to do?

Jen's Story

Jen, a pastor, was well acquainted with the superhero mentality. She recalled a time early in her ministry when she was working part-time in the church while dealing with a beloved family member's terminal illness. "I was over-functioning all over the place, trying to keep everyone in the family sane, trying to do everything. I was really angry at everything that was beyond my control, and I tried to fix it, but that just made it worse." She paused, and a wry smile crept over her face. "I finally went to a therapist who said, 'You might have some issues with boundaries.'"

Jen's unmet need was to be a fixer—the one who solved all the problems. Upon therapy and reflection, she realized something powerful: Her ministry was not effective if she was not allowing others to find and use their gifts for the kingdom. When she did everything herself instead of delegating, she denied others an opportunity to grow while she became angrier and more exhausted. This wasn't anything close to the ministry she or God envisioned.

The core of the superhero mentality is the need to rescue others—to save them from their pain. It's human nature to avoid pain because it is unpleasant and uncomfortable. That's what makes it pain. For those with empathetic and caring dispositions, seeing others in pain is almost intolerable. It creates pain within yourself to bear witness to theirs. It also triggers your own pain, which sometimes produces feelings of overwhelming psychological distress.

Since that distress is unconscious, you don't really know how to put it into words. You simply react. The 911 text bomb? It's the ultimate trigger of the superhero mentality. But did the person on the other end of the text *really* need to be rescued?

Or were you trying to rescue yourself?

Friend, if you can relate to this, please know that I am not judging. I am writing this chapter from a place of deep compassion because I've struggled with the superhero mentality my entire career. When I suffered my first bout of

> We already have a superhero. His name is Jesus.

burnout in my midtwenties as a social worker, I had to look at myself and figure it out. Here's what I learned: Pain is one of your best teachers. It forces you to look at what's real and what's not and to make healthier decisions. You can ignore pain for a long time, pushing it down way deep. But eventually, it will rise to the surface and force you to deal with it. And when it does, it can erupt in unpleasant and unpredictable ways, like a major health, employment, or relationship crisis.

The good news is that we already have a superhero. His name is Jesus.

> We also have joy with our troubles, because we know that these troubles produce patience. And patience produces character, and character produces hope. And this hope will never disappoint us, because God has poured out his love to fill our hearts. He gave us his love through the Holy Spirit, whom God has given to us.
>
> When we were unable to help ourselves, at the right time, Christ died for us, although we were living against God. Very few people will die to save the life of someone else. Although perhaps for a good person someone might possibly die. But God shows his great love for us in this way: Christ died for us while we were still sinners (Romans 5:3-8 NCV).

Jesus entered into your distress and pain, and he died to save you. Please note: *Jesus* is the one who died for *you*. He never asked you to kill yourself trying to rescue others, because that was his job. He loves you, and he loves those you care about. He sees your pain, and he is equipped to deal with it. He's the only true superhero.

> "I'm real clear that there is a Messiah and that I'm not him."

Wouldn't it be great to let him free you from your pain before you create your own crisis?

That's what Jen did. Look at her awesome takeaway from her burnout experience—this mantra now frames her ministry: "I'm real clear that there is a Messiah and that I'm not him."

What's the Real Deal?

Earlier in this chapter, you thought about the expectations you may have had before entering your profession. Did you learn anything about yourself that you weren't aware of before? If you need a little bit more time to reflect, take it now. Expectations and needs run deep, and it can take some time for them to rise to the surface.

This is a lot, Amy. Now that I know, how do I fix it?

Women and Men

Research indicates that people working in the helping professions (health care, teaching, social work, ministry, and so on) tend to burn out more often than others do. In fact, most of the professional and academic literature on burnout is written for people in these professions. The common thread among them is the desire to help others. In its healthiest form, this expectation is altruistic. In its unhealthy form, this expectation creates a distorted view of one's abilities. It is impossible to rescue, fix, or save everyone 100 percent of the time. (Did I really just need to write that? Actually, yes I did. I needed to hear it too!)

The superhero mentality is usually easier to see in women than in men. It's harder for women to acknowledge their need to rescue; they see themselves as nurturing and compassionate. Women feel a pull to nurture, so they may mistake rescuing for nurturing.

Men tend to be natural problem solvers and fixers. Sometimes men feel a lot of responsibility riding on their shoulders, so their natural reaction is to man up and take care of things. But sometimes this approach overlooks the entire situation or the feelings of others.

Both women and men can experience deep frustration and fatigue if they continue trying to rescue people. And for both women and men, the key is *awareness* because it is the first step to freedom. How does the superhero mentality manifest for you?

I have great news for you. You can address unfulfilled expectations and overcome the superhero mentality. It's not easy, because it is core psychological work, but it's doable and definitely worth the time and effort. You're already on the path; the first step was to identify your unfulfilled expectations in your work.

Next, identify some ways *I need, or else* drives you. Does it lead you to expect certain behaviors from yourself or other people? You might be surprised by what comes up. Just go with it! No judgment; work on accepting yourself even if you don't like what comes up. Later, you will have the opportunity to critically think about that need and make some changes. For now, just write down what you become aware of, and spend some time in reflection. Is this need something that you want to control your life? Can this need be met in other ways? How does Jesus want to meet this need for you instead of you unconsciously striving to meet it for yourself?

Overcome the Superhero Mentality

1. Start by identifying your unfulfilled expectations.
2. Identify the *I need, or else* drive that frames your expectations for behavior (yours and others).
3. Identify what cannot be changed in your current situation.
4. Renegotiate your expectations for your work.
5. Identify areas of personal pain, consider how they shaped your former expectations, and begin to resolve that pain through appropriate spiritual, psychological, or relational support.

Now shift your thoughts to reflect on your current work situation. What can you change, and what can't you change? You can either change the environment to meet your expectations, or you can change your expectations to meet the environment.

Let's unpack the first option. This could work if you are the boss or you have complete, independent control over everything. But the minute other people are involved, you would be seen as a control freak. People would do what you told them to out of fear and not out of respect. How would that work out for you?

Now let's consider the second option. This one feels defeating and maybe even like a cop-out. It's certainly disappointing because you won't always get what you want. However, in the long run, it teaches you to let go and allow situations to unfold, reducing your emotional energy spent feeling responsible for things you're not actually responsible for while giving you the opportunity to work on healing your deeper pain.

I vote for the second option! (That was Freudenberger's vote also.)

I love the Serenity Prayer by Reinhold Niebur because it so beautifully sums up this process:

> God, grant me the serenity to accept the things I
>   cannot change,
> Courage to change the things I can,
> And the wisdom to know the difference.[1]

This prayer is so simple, and it exactly reflects the process of renegotiating the faulty expectations around your work. You take stock of what you can realistically control, or what is yours to control, and you let go of what you can't. You are responsible only for what is yours; you are not responsible for anyone else's stuff. Maintaining this mindset can be difficult or even heart-wrenching, but it shows honor and respect for others and allows them to take care of their own business in their own way and in their own time.

You also get to trust that the real Superhero is at work here too. Because he is.

Rest and Reconnect

Let's revisit your unfulfilled expectations. How have they contributed to your burnout? Be specific. How can you renegotiate your expectations to fit your current reality? Write out specific statements. For example:

- I expect myself to adhere to a schedule, but I know that my colleagues do not share this value. Therefore, I expect that our team meetings will probably begin at least ten minutes late. With this knowledge, I choose to have a good attitude instead of becoming frustrated and withdrawing emotionally.
- I expect myself to be prepared for client meetings, but I know that my clients sometimes won't run their preliminary data reports before our meetings. Therefore, I expect that I will likely need to teach clients how to prepare and what information I will need in order to use our time efficiently.

Sometimes you may be forced to make a hard decision if you are chronically unhappy and there isn't a way to renegotiate your expectations. Stay tuned for chapters 13 and 14, where we revisit vocational changes and calling.

Will's Story

Will was an adrenaline junkie. He chose to become a paramedic because he couldn't imagine being stuck in a desk job like his friends were. Besides, the work would keep him physically fit so he could enjoy his weekend extreme sports. He dreamed of hiking the Pacific Crest Trail (PCT), and being a paramedic would keep him in shape.

Will spent several years in a training program, and he was excited when he was offered a job with the local county search and rescue team right away. But within months, Will was tired and didn't want to go to work any longer. He hadn't realized that his shifts would be mostly at night in inclement weather. He was able to handle witnessing the trauma of the work, but his work just didn't feel...exciting.

Will had expected his work to provide the same adrenaline rush he experienced on the weekends. Once he was able to get real about his work, he renegotiated his expectations. His job wasn't going to be thrilling all the time; there would be a lot of sitting around and waiting, paperwork, and working in difficult conditions. But it would provide him with the resources to do the things he loved. Will's change came when he was able to accept his current work conditions and intentionally create adrenaline and excitement outside of work. He set a goal of hiking the PCT the very next summer, and he used his downtime at work to plan the trip and get advice from his buddies.

The job never changed, but Will's perspective did. And so did his burnout.

Chapter 7 Key Points

- Burnout comes from unfulfilled expectations.
- The superhero mentality is a common unrealistic expectation.
- What are realistic expectations about your work?

Practice Being Free

Be still with God. Remove any distractions that may be present. Sit or lie comfortably, close your eyes, and open your hands. Pray or meditate:

God, I struggle with the superhero mentality. I acknowledge that you are God and I am not. You are the real superhero. Help me be free from the desire to always fix it. Help me accept the current reality of my work and to find healthy ways to meet my deepest needs.

This Week's To-Be List

_____

_____

_____

_____

_____

_____

_____

_____

_____

_____

_____

_____

_____

_____

_____

8

Be Held

Do not fear, for I am with you;
do not be dismayed, for I am your God
I will strengthen you and help you;
I will uphold you with my righteous right hand.

ISAIAH 41:10

magine your loneliest moment. It's a warm summer night—too hot to stay inside—so you sit on your porch in your baggy cutoffs. Because it's one of those moments where you can't contain it anymore. The facade, the mask you wear so brilliantly falls off, and the pain in your heart erupts into volcano-like sobs.

Because you are alone, you cry. And because *you are alone*, you cry.

You have nowhere else to go, nothing left. All you want is something to soothe your pain, to numb it or to take it away completely. Perhaps a cigarette? A pint of ice cream? A fifth of whiskey? Frantically, you search your phone for someone—anyone—who might give you a soft touch or a knowing smile. You have no idea how you are going to get through tonight, let alone how you will get through work tomorrow.

Because it's too much. It's all too much. Too much to process...and too much to do.

This chapter is about personal crisis and burnout. This topic is rarely mentioned in the research literature—if ever. Yet more than any other factor, a personal crisis affects your ability to manage your whole life. It especially affects your ability to function at work.

What Do You Mean by Crisis?

When I ask counseling clients about their personal experiences with crisis and trauma, they often say they haven't experienced any. But as we talk further, they mention things like divorce. Single parenting. A tragic automobile accident that happened years ago. Sometimes they don't mention things overtly but weave them into their stories, such as childhood abuse or living with a spouse who has a chronic substance abuse problem. They don't see a connection between these experiences and their current experience of burnout.

> A personal crisis affects your ability to manage your burnout.

I don't know if it's human nature to minimize trauma or if we just haven't learned to think of our experiences in this way. Perhaps our denial is a symptom of the superhero mentality we talked about in chapter 7, or perhaps we've just learned to tackle problems on our own. Regardless, crisis happens, and I can assure you that your own personal crisis has a huge influence on the burnout you are experiencing.

I'm going to share the stories of three workers experiencing personal crises. As you read them, can you identify with any of their experiences?

Maria

Maria is a single mother of two elementary schoolchildren. She loves being a mom more than anything else, and she stayed home with her children for many years. But when her husband left the marriage for another woman and moved to another state, Maria was forced to return to work. She has a two-year college degree in business and found a full-time job at a title company. But she works eight to five Monday through Friday, which means Maria doesn't see her kids until evening. Thankfully, her mother watches her kids after school, which cuts down on daycare costs. Even with child support, Maria is barely making it financially.

Maria feels afraid many nights. What if she loses her job? What if she is forced to make a difficult decision about health insurance? Even deeper, she grieves the loss of time spent with her children. Her biggest life dream was to be their mom—volunteering at their schools and going to their games. She can't do that now with her work schedule. Her only social outlet is her work, but her coworkers don't seem to want to listen anymore. And forget finding a special someone to help—there's no way she could trust a man after her husband's infidelity and abandonment.

Andres

Andres is married with three children. He works as a heavy equipment diesel mechanic, and he feels good about his skills and his ability to provide for his family. He has a quiet, kind personality and exemplifies a stellar work ethic. He shows up on time, does more than his fair share, and is well-respected among the guys.

One afternoon, one of the vehicles suddenly backfires. The sound is explosive, and the smell of diesel fuel wafts through the air. Everyone but Andres laughs. In fact, Andres seems to have disappeared, and he is soon found curled up into a fetal position, shaking, underneath a dump truck. His eyes are glazed, and he unresponsive. When the guys confirm he isn't hurt, they start joking. "What's the matter, Andres—can't take a little heat?" Andres unfurls in anger and punches the guy standing next to him square in the jaw.

That afternoon, Andres, sitting in front of the HR manager, is terminated for his behavior. "We have a zero-tolerance policy for violence," she says. But she forgot to ask Andres *why* he may have lost it like he did. As a stand-up guy, Andres never felt the need to talk about his personal life, including the fact that he is a former US Army reservist with two deployments to Iraq.

Joel

Joel is a graduate student who has one more year until he earns his degree. He's married to the love of his life, who works as a substance abuse counselor. After many years of trying to get pregnant, they were successful, but sadly, his wife miscarried at week 16. The loss devastated both of them.

Joel continues to go to class and complete his schoolwork, but he looks like he is barely surviving. He is tired and haggard, and he's lost his zeal for his studies and his future career. Other students are beginning to worry about him, even suggesting that he look into taking antidepressant medication.

Maria, Andres, and Joel are each experiencing a personal crisis. Maria is experiencing a crisis of overwhelming personal stressors. Her work and emotional load have brought her to a breaking point and have begun to affect her sleep and mental health. In addition, she feels horribly lonely and bereft of a support system. Andres is experiencing PTSD from his military deployment. Even though he is able to keep it together 99 percent of the time, his trauma is triggered without warning with serious consequences. Joel is experiencing deep grief and loss, combined with the additional stressors of graduate school.

Each of these individuals might say, "Hey, I'm fine." Or others around them might say, "That's life." But pain is pain. Personal stressors, untreated mental health issues (including substance abuse), and grief and loss often go unrecognized as they pile up. They hide just beneath the surface, only to rise when triggered. Or they can fester for years, creating even more depression, anxiety, and burnout.

Have you experienced a personal crisis? Could a crisis possibly be contributing to your burnout? Take a few moments to think about it.

Women and Men

Men and women experience crisis differently, especially at work. By nature, women tend to be more relational and seek social support when they experience crisis. This quality could result in women coworkers developing deeper relationships, having lunch together, or verbally processing their personal experiences. This helps women work through crisis together, but women need to be careful not to focus so much on their personal lives that their work environment suffers or they don't complete their tasks.

In contrast, men tend to shut down emotionally in crisis, or they deny its presence altogether. Men tend to have a strong sense of duty, so they may work longer hours to compensate for personal crises that may hurt their family's financial well-being. Unfortunately, society teaches men not to express their emotions—except anger or aggression. Coworkers rarely consider that a man might be expressing anger because he is feeling sad or fearful.

Both men and women are likely to seek coping mechanisms during crisis. These may be positive (exercise, spiritual practices) or negative (substance abuse, irresponsible sexual behaviors). Try to be mindful of this if you feel judgmental or frustrated with a coworker who is going through a personal crisis. If you are concerned about a colleague, reach out to them. Try to see the deeper pain beneath their behavior. Often a simple gesture—like a smile or an offer to bring them coffee—can make them feel seen and cared for. Finally, encourage your colleagues to get help if they need it, and do what you can to destigmatize the need for extra support if you hear rumors from others at work.

It's easy to ignore the lasting effects of a crisis. It's easy to push it aside, minimize it, or even be in complete denial about it. Caretakers often rise to a crisis by taking care of everyone else and set their own needs aside. This is nothing to be ashamed about; it is a natural way that our psyche protects itself from pain.

But the problem is that pain and trauma eventually settle deep in your heart and body. Even when unrecognized, it will fester there until it is dealt with. Often it comes out in symptoms that make up the syndrome we know as burnout.

A Time-Out

If you have experienced a personal crisis, please call it what it is—*a crisis*. Simply naming the crisis will change the way you view it. It also helps you recognize that your needs are greater than usual right now.

It is so important that you attend to your needs. So very important.

I know you need a paycheck. I know there are bills to pay, kids to parent, and all kinds of things you need to show up for. But you would take all the time you need to heal after a major surgery, wouldn't you? Your emotional heart needs that same kind of care.

So give yourself permission to take a time-out. Is there any way that you can...

- Reduce your workload?
- Lighten your work duties for a while? (For example, could you trade a task that stresses you out with another coworker?)
- Go part-time for a few weeks?
- Take a leave of absence? (Check to see whether you qualify for Family Medical Leave Act.)

- Take a sabbatical?
- Find a different job?
- Quit working altogether?

If none of these suggestions is an option, then at the very least, you need one chunk of time per week (ideally once a day) for FAPT, or "fall-apart time." FAPT includes wearing your comfiest clothes, tending to nothing but yourself, and being with anything and anyone that comforts you. You can cry, you can stay in bed, or you can just lie on the carpet and stare at the ceiling if you need to.

Please schedule some FAPT right now. I'm serious. Get out your day planner and write it in. In color, highlighted. Do FAPT for as long as you need to. How will you know when you don't need it anymore? When you can get through a day or a week without crying.

FAPT is so important for your healing. Trust me. You will thank me later.

A Warm Embrace

You, on your porch. Alone. Wanting something or someone to soothe your pain.

If you are quiet and allow your anxiety to settle, a deeper feeling emerges. It's a longing attached to a face. Your heart brings a person to the surface of your consciousness. It's the one person who always sees you. Your person.

Our God of relationship designed something beautiful called attachment. As children, we attach to a primary caregiver. That's the person who kisses your scrapes, takes care of the bullies at school, and nourishes you with snuggles and hot cocoa. It's the first person to whom you wanted to show off the best of you. "Mommy, look at me!

Papa, watch this!" Attachment was designed this way so that we could experience love. In the safety of that love, we grow into the best version of ourselves as whole people, as God envisioned us to be.

As an adult, you transfer this love attachment to your most intimate relationship. You receive your deepest comfort from this person. This person is safe. They feel like home. They are the one you love.

Who is your person?

You are still alone, but now you aren't. Because now you can sense the presence of your person. Their arms wrapping around you, their eyes pouring love into you so deeply, right into the depths of your soul. Smiling at you warmly. Desiring to know and experience every part of you even though now your sobs have become the snot-flinging, chest-heaving, mascara-streaking kind. This definitely is not your prettiest or most put-together moment, but you have never felt more wanted.

Some years ago, I experienced an extended season of personal crisis. I'll spare you the details, but in short, I desperately wanted to have a family. I was working several jobs to make ends meet and to provide the funds to create a family through fertility treatment or adoption. Throughout that tired, dark season, I lost eight children in eight years. I honestly felt like I could not go on.

But I had to go on. Bills needed to be paid, ministry needed to be done, and students needed to be taught. So I got up every day and tried to put on my game face. Truth be told, my game face looked more like the fog above my head had exploded into a ball of gray slime that constantly sagged my eyes down and twisted my lips into a perpetual snarl. I was the walking embodiment of burnout. I could barely hold it together at work.

One night, in a Bible study of all places, I just let it all go. All the trying to be nice and keeping it together like a good Christian should...I just sat there listlessly. I wasn't done with God, but I was done believing that he would give me anything good. Instead of praying like the others, I dropped my head into my hands and cried.

And then I saw Jesus.

Now, in my profession, seeing Jesus could be equated to having a psychotic episode. But I knew I wasn't psychotic because all I felt was peace. His arms were outstretched. He didn't say a word, but he didn't have to. His eyes said it all. Radiating from them were...

love

compassion

warmth

forgiveness

acceptance

understanding

Divine love. I had been a Christian my whole life and read about God's love, but I had never experienced it like that. So fully, so radically. It transformed me, and it transformed my faith.

Divine love transforms everything.

For the first time, I was allowed. Allowed to be me in my most vulnerable, helpless, can't-do-it-anymore state. And I let myself off the hook at work. I let "good enough" be good enough. Was I at my best? Absolutely not. Did things slide? Absolutely. But by allowing myself to focus on healing my personal crisis, eventually, I got to my best again.

Remember how I mentioned "allowing" in chapter 2? As Christians, we sometimes get such a mixed message about allowing. *You are loved, you are saved...but only after you do X, Y, and Z.* That's called a double bind, which means you're not going to win either way, and it's crazy-making. There's no X, Y, or Z with Jesus. You are always allowed to *be* without doing anything. You are allowed to grieve. You are allowed to cry. To be you, at your best and at your worst. It's the deepest love that exists.

No more double binds, friend. Instead, this is what you need to hear, and I'm saying it to you now. Let Jesus knit it deep within your heart:

You are allowed to fall apart.

You are allowed to be angry.

You are allowed to cry and cry and cry. And even swear in the middle of those cries.

You are allowed to ask really, really hard questions. Like *Why?* and *What for?* and *What is the meaning of this?*

You are allowed to have needs and to do whatever it takes to get those needs met.

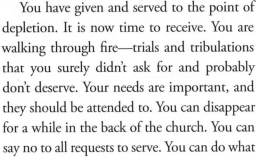

You have given and served to the point of depletion. It is now time to receive.

You have given and served to the point of depletion. It is now time to receive. You are walking through fire—trials and tribulations that you surely didn't ask for and probably don't deserve. Your needs are important, and they should be attended to. You can disappear for a while in the back of the church. You can say no to all requests to serve. You can do what you need to do to take care of yourself and heal. For as long as it takes.

It is now time to be wrapped in a warm embrace. Whether you receive that from a human person or not, you are seen by Jesus. He will always show up for you; he will always be your person. His presence is with you on that porch and every day everywhere else too. Wrapping around you. Accepting you. Wanting you. Allowing you.

You are home, child. Because wherever you are, Jesus is also.

Be held.

When It's Time for Professional Help

Your personal crisis may have reached the point where you need some professional help. How do you know whether you can handle it on your own or if you need assistance? The answer is simple: Get help when you can't manage anymore. If your work, relationships, or physical health has become impaired, it's time to call a counselor or therapist.

If you or a loved one are experiencing any of the following, please get help immediately:

- suicidal thoughts or plans
- dissociation (disconnection from your thoughts, feelings, memories, and so on)
- psychosis
- a desire or plan to hurt others
- addiction, including gambling and unwanted sexual behaviors

Find a licensed professional counselor or therapist, social worker, or psychologist. It's fine to seek spiritual support as well, but make sure that those helping you are trained in advanced mental health care.

Chapter 8 Key Points

- Personal stressors, trauma, grief, and loss play key roles in burnout.
- It is important to take time out during a personal crisis.
- You are seen, loved, and held by Jesus.

Practice Being Held

Be still with Jesus. Remove any distractions that may be present. Sit or lie comfortably, close your eyes, and open your hands. Pray or meditate:

Jesus, I know you are here with me. I know you can see my deepest pain. I know that you love me and that you care. I don't know the answers right now, but I don't need to. Just hold me.

This Week's To-Be List

_____

_____

_____

_____

_____

_____

_____

_____

_____

_____

_____

_____

_____

_____

_____

_____

_____

9

Be Edified

*Let us therefore make every effort to do what
leads to peace and to mutual edification.*

ROMANS 14:19

I just looked at my Instagram feed, and here's what I saw:

Five vacation photos posted by two different friends. A photo from one of my girlfriends who has run a half-marathon every month for 40 consecutive months (you go, girl). Seven pictures of food and ten pictures of diet and exercise ads, all in slick copy and posted by people I don't even know. A few topical postings by Christian authors and speakers. One post by a tattoo artist I follow (don't ask). And too many "rah-rah" posts to count—inspirational posts to be all I can be, do more, and to basically be amazing.

Oh my goodness. I'm tired just from all that scrolling.

Also, now I feel sort of...inadequate. My goals are not nearly so impressive: Getting in my morning workout, packing a healthy lunch, and being on time for my ten o'clock meeting. If I were to go on vacation and eat awesome food, I think I'd be so excited, I wouldn't have time to post it on Instagram. And I surely wouldn't post a photo of my tattoo!

Do you ever feel like everyone else's lives are so much better than yours? Like they have it all together and you don't? I'm pretty sure God delights in us living life to the fullest, but sometimes seeing everyone else at their best makes you feel like you are continually stuck at your worst.

Honestly, I think the rah-rah messages get me down the most. You know, what all the inspirational motivators are saying. Those messages really frustrate me even though I know it's absolutely not their intention. In some ways, I love them because they ignite energy to start a new project or to think about my life a little differently. But in other ways, I hear their stories and see what they've accomplished, but I know they are one in ten million, and my life isn't like theirs. But yet I still compare their lives with mine, and I eventually end up feeling more discouraged.

> Discouragement
> is the liner on
> the trash can
> of burnout.

Discouragement is definitely not a feeling that helps you make positive life changes. Discouragement is more like the liner on the trash can of burnout. It slows you down until you just can't do any more. And then you feel even more pressure to get yourself together.

How do you think that pressure contributes to your burnout? (Hint: It does, a lot.)

If you are taking stock of your work and career right now, and I'm assuming you are since you're reading this book, wouldn't you like to find a way to get rid of your burnout and manage the rest of your work and life in a way that is encouraging and invigorating rather than discouraging?

It's not going to happen by increasing your so-called amazingness and then frantically working yourself to death. It comes through a quiet knock at your back door; it arrives in a way that is more comfortable and familiar. It's going to come through your heart.

Emotional Intelligence

Have you ever received a nasty-gram at work? You know, an email from someone who was just going on a rant? For some weird reason, when we humans talk with a keyboard, we can lose all sense of professionalism and decorum. Your workplace may be tolerant of "authentic" forms of communication—or your coworker may simply have poor emotional intelligence (EI).

EI is the ability to recognize and regulate emotions.[1] It helps you discern emotions, understand them, and manage them. Another way to conceptualize it is *emotional balance*—feeling your emotions authentically while keeping control of them and helping others to do the same. EI has been shown to be an effective tool for career success,[2] and some research suggests that it's even more powerful than cognitive intelligence.[3]

It's easy to lose it at work. Perhaps, like me, you've gotten angry or so overwhelmed that you had to take a break. Or more likely, you can keep it together at work, but your personal life is a train wreck. "Oh, Joe is such a great team player. But did you hear he almost got into a fistfight with another parent at Boy Scouts? Can't believe it—he's such a nice guy!" Yes, Joe is a great guy, but is he regulating his emotions consistently? Can he express what he needs and what he wants and be nice in all settings of his life?

I studied EI in my doctoral dissertation because I was interested in discovering whether it played a role in burnout. Not surprisingly, I found that people with higher EI experience lower burnout. It wasn't the only factor in burnout, but the correlation was strong enough to suggest that increasing EI could reduce burnout.

There's great news for people like Joe and the person at your work who sends the email rants. EI can be learned or improved. It's not a fixed trait like personality. In other words, if you don't have a high EI quotient yet, you can develop it. It's a great tool to manage not only your burnout but also your whole life.

High EI means that you are able to...

- recognize your feelings and communicate them to others in the moment
- manage your intense emotions (like anger) well enough to express how you are feeling without disrespecting or scaring others
- pay attention to the emotions of others and respond to those emotions rather than react to their negative behavior
- elicit helpful and positive emotions in others and help them to use those emotions to move toward their success
- understand the emotional climate of a meeting, workplace, or environment and manage it appropriately
- de-escalate situations that are emotionally out of control

Do you have these skills right now? If not, does EI sound like something you want to develop?

Got EI?

Look again at the bulleted list of traits of high EI. This is not a comprehensive list by any means, but it gives you an idea of how to develop EI in your own life. The key is to develop awareness and to use strategies to regulate your emotions.

I teach this skill to my counseling clients because it is foundational for achieving emotional balance. Here are a few ideas to help you develop EI:

- Learn the names of emotions and begin to name them in your own experience, such as, "I feel disappointed," or "I feel elated." This will be harder if you have not learned to express yourself emotionally or if emotional expression has never been safe and acceptable. Start by naming emotions to yourself, either in your thoughts or by writing them down. When that feels comfortable, find a trusted friend or two, and begin sharing your feelings with them. Gradually, it will become easier for you to express emotions to others.

- When you are experiencing intense emotions, such as anger or fear, practice taking a time-out. Find a place to be alone. Take deep breaths until you can communicate your emotions respectfully and safely.

- Practice identifying and reflecting other people's emotions. "I sense you are feeling relaxed after the weekend," or "I wonder if you are feeling confused about this project" will go a long way in increasing rapport.

- If a situation feels tense, try to identify how people are feeling, and then respond to that feeling rather than to their behavior. "Isla, I see that you feel very strongly about this, but I wonder if perhaps you are also feeling that your efforts on this project are not being acknowledged. I want you to know how much I appreciate your contributions. Can we take a few minutes to calm down and then regroup to find a solution together?"

Women and Men

Are there differences in gender and EI? The research indicates no, women and men possess and interact with equal emotional intelligence.[4] My dissertation also confirmed this finding. However, research supports the common impression that women tend to recognize and respond to emotions better than men, which gives them an advantage in social interactions.[5] The setting significantly determines the way in which women and men interact emotionally. However, both genders can adapt based on the demands of the workplace.

Nurturing and child-rearing are more often done by women, and this caretaking role predisposes women to be more emotionally attuned. However, this could cause women to interact in ways that are not appropriate for the workplace, especially with people, projects, and environments that are dominated by cognition. Women may need to develop a "thicker skin" and to learn to let things go if they tend to be emotionally sensitive. (Sorry, not sorry if that offended you—let's start practicing right now!) It's important to mention that women are not predisposed to always be soft, sweet, and gentle...there are so many wonderful examples of assertive and successful women in the workplace. I'd guess that their EI scores are pretty high and that they have a great deal of empathy as well.

Providing and protecting are more often performed by men, and this provider role predisposes men to be more aggressive and competitive. It works well most of the time, as long as that aggression can be expressed productively. Interestingly, men can develop very good emotional recognition and communication skills if they perceive that these abilities will get them ahead in the workplace. It just needs to be framed in a way that they understand, which is typically by motivation of a prize. A little competition never hurts anyone, does it?

One challenge is learning to use the emotional style that the setting requires. You may find that your workplace demands a certain style of communication and emotional interaction, whereas your home life will ask for another. It may help you to think about the emotional climate in each of your life settings and practice functioning in each setting accordingly. Take some time thinking through—and practicing—how you want to interact in each setting. Give yourself time as you transition between each setting, and decide how you want to interact when you arrive.

Be Edified

Edification is moral instruction that is based on God's Word. It is a tool to encourage you toward a righteous and abundant life. The external messages—social media, your boss, or even well-meaning Christians that don't quite get it—pale in comparison to the edification God has for you.

Here's a verse that translates to an important principle for burnout prevention: "The LORD detests dishonest scales, but accurate weights find favor with him" (Proverbs 11:1).

What could this verse possibly have to do with emotional intelligence and edification? Simple—it has to do with living a balanced life.

In biblical times, people bought and sold by weight. For kicks, let's say a pound of flour cost five cents. If the scales were weighted improperly, the buyer would be cheated out of some of their flour. It would not likely be a lot, but the seller could rig the scales just enough so that over many sales, they would grow rich. This proverb is saying that God hates cheating. But God loves to see people interacting and using their gifts together; he loves the process of bartering and trading, which is part of doing business or working.

This proverb applies to your life too. How do you cheat yourself out of an abundant life? Do you weigh the scales of your life activities unfairly, such as working too much or spending more energy on certain activities to the detriment of others? How might achieving emotional balance help you deal with each area of your life in a peaceful, productive way?

Rest and Reconnect

What would a photo of you being your most emotionally intelligent self look like?

Close your eyes, take a breath, and let the image come to you. Now smile because...I want you to take this photo and post it on social media today! (I dare you.)

True Amazingness

Love the touchy-feely stuff, Amy, but what does EI have to do with my burnout?

We clearly know that people with higher EI are more successful at work. If you want to be successful in your work and career, EI will help you achieve that goal. The people around you will be grateful too, and your relationships are likely to improve. But this book is about burnout; resolving your burnout is your main goal right now. So here's the big reason that developing EI will help your burnout:

EI will help you to regulate and cope with your emotions.

Burnout is a maladaptive state of the heart more than a maladaptive state of the mind. Think about it—the core experience of burnout is emotional exhaustion and the loss of personal meaning. Yes, you also experience physical and mental symptoms (like weight gain and reduced concentration), but they are not the underlying issue. If they were, those latter symptoms would resolve after a nice, long vacation.

Would a vacation solve everything for you right now? If it would, then please put this book down and head to the airport! But you and I both know that a vacation probably won't permanently heal your emotional exhaustion and fix your existential crisis. You got in this state by overusing your mind to the detriment of using your heart. You have *forgotten* to use your heart. You have forgotten to feel and to honor your feelings. You have forgotten to communicate your feelings and receive validation and affirmation from people who love you.

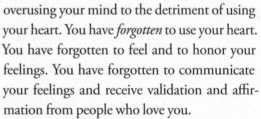

> Burnout is a maladaptive state of the heart more than a maladaptive state of the mind.

No shame in this, friend. The demands of your workplace are great. Then you go home to all the amazingness you see on social media and TV. Always being amazing is a tough gig. All those messages eventually filter through your mind and plant feelings of inadequacy and despair into your heart.

Instead, you can learn to regulate your negative feelings and move toward feelings that are more positive. You can identify your feelings and allow yourself to feel them (all without judging them), and when you do, you will naturally begin to accept yourself. At the same time, you can evaluate which feelings work or don't work for you, keeping what you want and getting rid of what you don't. You develop a balanced emotional state, honoring your gifts, your current situation (including your limits), and your unique calling. And guess what? You do the same for others.

Now *that's* truly amazing!

I hope chapters 7, 8, and 9 have helped you reconnect with yourself. The areas we discussed—the superhero mentality, personal crises, and emotional intelligence—are by no means the only things that predispose you to burnout. They just happen to be the most relevant to the modern workplace. If you know other areas that are pertinent, would you take a minute now to contact me at my website? I'd love to hear your personal story. You can find me online at www.amyohana.com. Don't worry—I'll never share your story without your permission. I'd just love to hear how you have grown through your journey of restoration from burnout.

We're transitioning now to the next section of the book, where we'll discover how to reconnect with our work. We'll focus on re-creating your relationship with work in productive, healthy ways, which is guided by the fourth intention of burnout resolution. I'm excited about this part because it inspires you to think about your work and career in fresh ways.

Rest and Reconnect

Another quality that beautifully synchronizes with EI is empathy. Empathy is the ability to feel what another person is feeling and respond affirmatively to that feeling. Emotionally intelligent, empathic people can be the most caring, competent, and successful people in the workplace. They are fantastic leaders because they can see and capitalize on the strengths of those they work with.

Interestingly, people with high EI and low empathy can have sociopathic traits because they can manipulate other's emotions to achieve their goals. That is important to mention because sociopaths comprise between 3 and 10 percent of the population and typically choose careers in leadership. Yes, they definitely are in the workplace! Sociopathology is especially common in CEOs, politicians, and sadly, the clergy—influential careers.

You are likely to encounter a leader or coworker with high or low EI as well as high or low empathy in your daily experience at work. How will you discern who is who? Review the bulleted list on page 124 for telltale signs.

For your personal growth: How can you practice empathy in the next hour? Find someone near you and give it a try!

Chapter 9 Key Points

- Cultural messages to be amazing lead to discouragement and burnout.
- Emotional intelligence is an effective way to cope with burnout.
- Learn to live in a balanced state that is uniquely you.

Practice Being Edified

Spend some time with God. Remove any distractions that may be present. Sit or lie comfortably, close your eyes, and open your hands. Pray or meditate:

God, I get discouraged by all the messages I see that make me feel as if I need to be amazing. Help me discern your true message for me. Give me the skills to cope with my burnout in healthy ways. Increase my empathy and love, and help me receive these in return.

Common Emotions in the Workplace

Refer to this list if you need a little help putting your feelings into words. This list is by no means exhaustive—there are hundreds of emotions! I've selected emotions that you are likely to find at work. This list will give you a good start for having those difficult, emotionally sensitive conversations at work.

acknowledged	hopeful	perplexed	relieved
affirmed	hungover	hurt	sad
aggressive	confident	hysterical	satisfied
angry	courageous	indifferent	sheepish
anxious	curious	interested	smug
assertive	disappointed	kind	sympathetic
apologetic	determined	loaded	tired
bored	excited	lonely	thoughtful
cautious	exhausted	meditative	unplugged
concentrating	frustrated	optimistic	valued
guilty	mischievous	puzzled	vulnerable
happy	negative		

Challenge yourself to use at least a few of these feeling words whenever you talk with your colleagues tomorrow!

This Week's To-Be List

The Five Intentions of Burnout Resolution

I.
I will practice stillness so God can
restore my soul.

II.
I will seek connection with God,
myself, and my work.

III.
I will cultivate awareness of who I am,
where I am, and what I want to be.

IV.
**I will take consistent steps to
promote well-being in my work.**

V.
I will focus on who I am to *be*,
not what I am to *do*.

10

Be Satisfied

You open your hand and satisfy the
desires of every living thing.

PSALM 145:16

t must be the hundredth time you've looked at your phone. You've been expecting it—*the text*. Communication from your lover about when and where to meet. Wednesday afternoon and stuck at work, it's all you can think about. You guys do this; this is your thing. With out-of-control schedules, you have to make time for your trysts. Otherwise, it would never happen.

You check your phone again. No text yet.

It's been a while. You close your eyes and remember the last time—how it felt to join together and feel a oneness that you never knew existed. With shaking fingers, you attempt to finish typing your email, but your eyes dissociate from the screen. Anticipation curves your lips into a sweet smile. The tension is almost as good as the consummation.

Still no text.

You recall something your lover did last time, and you moan—softly so that your coworkers won't hear. Joy rises from your naval, kindling the flames already licking the inside of your belly. Ardent yearning floods energy through your veins, bleeding into your sinews and bones. Every part of your being is reposed into delicious ache.

Finally, the text.

You drop everything and go.

If you thought that burnout was a boring topic, well, this chapter is a game changer. Because we are going to talk about sex and love and passion. It's going to get hot, baby!

In Love

Are you passionately in love with your work?

Amy, this is getting a little weird. As if my work were a love affair!

The idea of work creating a love triangle is not so strange. Check out some famous quotes by recognized career experts. "Follow your bliss," wrote Joseph Campbell, professor of literature and well-known author. "Do what you love, the money will follow," Marsha Sinetar wrote in a 1987 book with the same title. I've definitely heard that one! How about this one—"The only way to do great work is to love what you do. If you haven't found it yet, keep looking. Don't settle. As with all matters of the heart, you'll know when you find it" (Steve Jobs).

This sounds a bit like love to me!

There are many types of love; it comes in many forms. Christians are encouraged to practice a higher form of love called agape, which is the self-sacrificial love of Jesus. There is eros, the root of the word "erotic," which is passionate love, or love filled with desire. There is philia, or affectionate love, which is the love shared between friends. You may have heard of platonic love, which also describes friendship, derived from the writings of Plato. *Storgē* is a Greek word that describes the love of familiarity and attachment, such as in parent-child and other family relationships. *Philautia*, another Greek word, represents self-love—the kind of regard one has for oneself, especially to grow. (Reading this book is an example of your own *philautia*!) A few others aren't as well-known, and I'm sure you've heard about the types of love before. But here's a question you may never have considered:

What type of love is most common at work?

Reread the introduction to this chapter and I'll give you one guess.

If you guessed eros, you are correct. The energy for work comes from eros. Yes, eros is associated with romantic and sexual behavior, but those are its manifestations and not its root. Eros is derived from the Greek verb *eírō*, which means "to tie, join, fasten, or string together." The intention of eros is oneness, which represents the Holy Trinity and mirrors the kind of relationship God desires to have with you.

The energy of eros is passion. It is what we mean when we say "in love"—love that is all-consuming. It flows through every part of your being, magnetically drawing you to oneness in heart, body, and mind with the beloved. It's the kind of love you don't choose, because it chooses you. The kind of love that is irrational, unreasonable, and often uncontrollable. The kind of love that fuels you, that ignites your fever and fervor. It's love that consumes you with burning and yearning until the only thing you can do to satisfy it is to engage.

Eros is the coach revving up players for the championship game.

Eros is the creative waking up at night and staying up till morning painting the dream.

Eros is the entrepreneur who works 70 hours a week to meet a community need with an innovative service.

God is the full embodiment of love, including eros. Eros is the most intense form of love because it is hot, burning passion. From eros come two important entities: creativity and productivity. God set these entities as a foundation of work. Through creativity, God formed the universe. Through productivity, God sustains the universe. Eros is the love-energy God used to design you, me, and the world around us; eros is the love-energy that God expends to fulfill us.

> From eros come creativity and productivity— the love-energy required to find fulfillment in work.

All of the burnout resources available today share this one theme: You have lost your passion, and that's why you are burned out; you need to get your passion back. Yes, that message is true, but it's not the complete answer. When you understand exactly what that passion is, where it comes from, and how to engage it—well, everything changes. That passion is eros. It comes from God. Its purpose is to create, sustain, and satisfy, ultimately bringing things together in oneness. And to engage it? Read on.

Is It Only Eros?

If there are many forms of love, does only eros show up at work? The answer is no, work can embody all forms of love. For example, you can have a lunchtime Bible study (*philia*), take your family out for dinner on payday (*storgē*), or increase your self-esteem by learning a new skill (*philautia*). However, with eros, you experience passion in and for your work.

What are some ways that you can give, receive, and express love at work today?

Sex, Romance, and Work

Work and sex. You probably never thought of those two coupling, but they go together like the *arpa jarocha* and "La Bamba." You can't have one without the other. I told you this chapter was going to get a little McSteamy!

When you are burned out, your eros is blocked or misdirected. Your creativity and productivity at work smolder and eventually die, leaving you exhausted, disillusioned, and hopeless. Eventually, this state trickles into your personal life, your relationships, and your physical body. It's easy to shrug your shoulders and say, "I'm burned out," blaming something about your work. In reality, work is simply a stimulus. Failure of eros response is the problem. The solution?

Release the eros within your heart, and then channel it into your work.

Easier said than done. The culture doesn't like this kind of terminology, especially in the workplace. There are fears about crossing boundaries and sexual misconduct, and rightly so. When it comes to romance and sex, Christian culture is stoic at best and downright suppressive at worst. But when you reframe the word "eros" as passion rather than sex or romance, it's acceptable. In fact, it makes a whole lot more sense. Release the *passion* in your heart, and then channel it into your work.

God is love, and he gave you love as a gift. It is okay to experience eros and to draw on it for work. In fact, that's one of the areas God wants you to use it! It looks different for each gender, which means that men and women will benefit from different eros-igniting strategies. Please note: What I've written below are generalities based on social norms and may or not describe individuals. Consider this information as a point to start a conversation rather than an absolute.

Men: Ignite Your Eros

Primarily, men first experience eros through the physical body, which is why they are stereotypically believed to have a higher sexual drive. Once activated in the body, men experience eros through their hearts and minds. It is for this reason that regular sex is so important to a man's success at work. His sexual fulfillment is the gatekeeper of his energy to go to work, deal with problems at work, and be productive.

A wife can be a big help in this area. A man needs to be encouraged to have a regular physical and sexual release, and it's important to note that he doesn't just need the release; he needs to be encouraged by his wife toward physical and sexual release. During intimacy, his wife must attend to his heart and mind just as much as his body. Due to gender socialization, sexual intimacy might be the only time a man feels safe expressing his emotions. When his wife desires and accepts all of him, a man feels seen, wanted, and appreciated—which then influences how he performs at work. When a man and his wife understand his needs for sex, vulnerability, and work, they can partner together toward his vocational success.

Of course, sex isn't the only way to engage the physical body. Exercise, sports, massage, outdoor hobbies, and physical labor are also effective. If a man's work predominately involves sitting at a desk for long periods of time, it is especially important to prioritize physical outlets during self-care. Even better, try to find time during the workday to engage the body. Start a lunchtime basketball league or take breaks outside.

When a man works and loves passionately, there is no stopping his potential for strength, courage, and compassion. Sex is so important, but it is a myth that men are only interested in sex. Men are very capable of experiencing eros through their hearts and minds. They love deeply; they just love differently than women do. Women can generate a man's love by making sure his efforts are valued and appreciated.

Women: Ignite Your Eros

Primarily, women first experience eros through the heart, which is why they are stereotypically more interested in romance. Once activated in the heart, women will experience eros through the mind and body. When a woman is in love with her work, her creativity heightens and her energy flows. This is how she integrates her femininity—metaphorically, she nurtures and gives birth to her work.

A woman needs to be encouraged to fall in love with her work. It seems like a mystical concept, but trust me, she will totally understand this: "Is there anything about work that you can fall in love with? Pour your energy into that." Women can always find something to love; that's how God wired them. Men can be instrumental in encouraging women to work according to their feminine nature. Women often fight to be recognized and respected in male-dominated workplaces. Men can back off, show respect, and let a woman's natural creative process take over. They can protect her productivity by supporting a task or project she is leading instead of challenging her or offering solutions she didn't ask for.

Empower a woman to work and love passionately, and there is no stopping her potential for creativity, beauty, and generativity. A nice side effect of a woman working in her full eros is that her sexual desire naturally increases when her heart and mind are filled with passionate love. That's a great thing for her *and* her husband!

The full satisfaction of eros is complete oneness in heart, body, and mind. This can include sex and romance, but it is not limited to it. If it's sex, it has to be great sex. Yes, you really did just read that correctly! It has to be *great, fulfilling sex.* Sex that satisfies only the body does not express eros. It might feel awesome—for a night. Then the longing in your heart pulls you straight back to another quick fix. It's exactly the same thing if you engage in romantic fantasy while watching Lifetime movies but let your body and appearance go. It might feel emotionally safe, but it will never fully satisfy eros. That's why it's even more important to spend time nurturing your marriage so that your intimacy—heart, body, mind, and soul—is complete and fulfilling.

You can experience eros in many ways. Think about some things you do every day that involve the heart, body, and mind. Perhaps jogging or yoga. An affirmation to your child and the hug shared afterward. Repairing an air conditioning unit while joking around with your buddy. In these moments, slow down and pay attention to how your heart fills and the energy you receive. This is eros. Passionate love. Release it again by pouring it back into the beloved—or your work.

You *Can* Get Satisfaction

I'm getting a little dizzy because of this hot topic and because I've been typing for quite a while. I keep thinking of Mick Jagger's "I can't get no satisfaction..." I'm thinking about your satisfaction—that is, your satisfaction with work.

Porn, Affairs, and Sexual Misconduct at Work

It's not a shocker that unwanted sexual behavior often starts at work. In fact, the use of pornography has been associated with men's perceived failure in work, and working women report higher instances of extramarital affairs. There is a lot of talk in Christian communities as to why this happens, such as the increased availability of porn through the internet or feminist ideology encouraging women into the workforce. Perhaps these factors are at play.

More likely, unwanted sexual behavior occurs because of blocked or misdirected eros. Eros needs to be ignited and experienced (in the heart, body, and mind) and then channeled into productive means, including work and family relationships. When done successfully, you improve your self-esteem, increase your productivity, and affair-proof your marriage.

Research verifies what I've found to be true in my experience with career and vocational counseling: When our work matches our values, we are much more likely to feel satisfied in our careers.[1] Your values are what is important or meaningful to you. If your work does not fulfill your values, you simply are not going to be happy.

What is most important to you? Close your eyes and take a moment to think about it.

I'll guess you had several images come to mind...perhaps your children or loved ones or something you want to have. Those are awesome things, but they are not your values. Values are deeper, sometimes unspoken, and often based on early learning. As we discussed in chapter 6, your values influence your beliefs, which in turn influence your thoughts. When you are unhappy in your work and don't know why, think about your values and how your work fulfills them. You might have one of those aha moments we therapists love so much.

Have you ever participated in a branding brainstorm session? Along with the mission and vision of the organization, you also can choose your core values. You can evaluate your unconscious values and replace them with values that you choose for yourself. Values typically are expressed in one or two words. In the workplace, they frame the entire way of being in that environment. Similarly, your personal core values frame your own entire way of being.

> When our work matches our values, we are much more likely to feel satisfied in our careers.

When you are consciously aware of and authentically living within your values, you experience incredible stability and drive. You know who you are and live out your true identity every day. Steve from chapter 4 is an example. He was unhappy and unsatisfied in his teaching career for years. Teaching fulfilled many of his values—but not the ones that were most important. Above all, he valued autonomy, flexibility, and helping others. His value of helping others was satisfied, but autonomy and flexibility were lacking. When he figured out what he valued most and found a career that matched it, he felt deeply satisfied.

What are your core personal values? Can you name your top three? How about your top ten? Again, take some time to reflect on this question. Identify them, write them down, and place the list somewhere you will see it often—at your desk, on the bathroom mirror, or in your car. Seeing them often reminds you to live authentically each day.

When you find work that matches your core values, your burnout dies, and your fulfillment thrives. Knowing your core values helps you make better decisions in your career development. Have you ever been to a job interview where they grilled you and then asked, "Do you have any questions for us?" Now your answer should be, "Why, yes I do—thank you for asking!" Then proceed to ask questions about the job or the organization to see if it is a good fit with your values. Values should guide all your career decisions, including quitting or staying at a job, advancement, your overall career trajectory, and the like.

It might surprise you to know that your satisfaction is one of God's values. I've never heard a sermon preached about this, but it's true. Look at Psalm 145:16: "You open your hand and satisfy the desires of every living thing."

God knows what is important to you. Of course he does—he created you! He's not a distant, stoic, joyless being. His heart is delighted to watch you embody passionate love at work and to see you satisfy your deepest desires.

As Christians, sometimes we miss the importance of satisfaction. You are encouraged to deny yourself. You get the sacrifice part, but somehow, it's not okay to be satisfied or to revel in pleasure. Sacrifice is good in its context, but it is not the fullness of God. The first story about God's work says, "God saw all he had made, and it was very good" (Genesis 1:31). God was satisfied with *his* work. So I'm going to take a wild leap and suggest that if God revels in his own satisfaction, you can too.

I'll ask you once again: Are you passionately in love with your work?

Can you imagine longing to engage with work just as you would a beloved?

If you are burned out, your love-energy for work has extinguished. Just as in a human relationship, your love for work dies when it is not tended to. Perhaps your love for your work began as a firestorm. Idealistic, you engaged wholeheartedly but found your energy quickly consumed, leaving you exhausted. You gave too much too soon, and now you don't know how to get that fire back.

Perhaps there are things that have eroded your connection with work, such as stressors or dealing with difficult people. You know deep in your heart that your job or career is "the one," but you need to reconnect.

Or perhaps the work you chose was all wrong from the beginning. You need to take stock of it and make some hard decisions, like making a radical change or ending it altogether. The chapters to come address each of these scenarios.

There is hope. It is possible to fall in love with work once again. It is possible to go to work each day with a song in your heart and fire in your belly. To wake up thinking, *Wow, I get to* [insert your cool thing here] *today.* To work hard, accomplish something, and then revel in the satisfaction of a job well done. And then get up and do it all again.

Passion. Satisfaction. Done over and over again, these lead to fulfillment.

It's as simple as opening your heart to receive God's love-energy and then burning it into your work. Eros has always been present—it just has to be ignited. Guess who has the match?

Getting Back to Fulfillment

In chapter 2, I promised to revisit the idea of fulfillment. I could write a whole book titled *Be Fulfilled* or talk about how helping people cultivate fulfillment is my life's passion. (I'm kinda crazy about it if you haven't figured that out.) Because fulfillment is just...so...big. There's no way to do it justice in so few words.

Here's what I'll do instead. In the next three chapters, you'll see fulfillment woven in like a thread. You already know that fulfillment is a state of being that is cultivated over time. We've been working up to this for a while, so now you are ready for the big reveal:

Fulfillment is the exact opposite of burnout.

Okay, so that wasn't such a big reveal. We talked about it in chapter 2, after all. But does it have more meaning for you now? When you are fulfilled, you are not burned out. To fix your burnout, move toward fulfillment. It's as simple as that. When you are fulfilled, you are less likely to burn out. Isn't it nice how that works out? (Again, no pun intended.)

Not surprisingly, the steps to fulfillment are the five intentions of burnout resolutions. So far, we've looked at the first three. Chapter 10 transitioned the book to intention number 4. In chapters 11 through 13, you'll reengage in ways that help you fall in love with work all over again and cultivate the fulfillment your soul craves.

Chapter 10 Key Points

- Eros—passionate love—is the love-energy that predominates work.

- Satisfaction is linked to how well your work matches your values.

- Fulfillment is generated by sustained satisfaction.

Practice Being Satisfied

Spend time with God. Remove any distractions that may be present. Sit or lie comfortably, close your eyes, and open your hands. Pray or meditate:

God, you passionately care about my satisfaction. Release that same passion within me. Help me channel that passion in productive, meaningful ways in my work.

Fall in Love: 10 Ways to Ignite Eros at Work

1. Pray and ask God to fill you with a passion for work. Keep praying until he does—he will be faithful.

2. Every day, fully engage your heart, body, and mind while working. Of course, the ways you do that will need to be unique to your specific situation and setting. Get creative!

3. Fuel some fire with friendly competition. Create a challenge with your coworkers or challenge yourself to perform well on a task. Celebrate afterward.

4. Work on projects or tasks that you most enjoy during hours of the day when you have the greatest energy.

5. Designate care of your physical body as one of your top daily priorities. This includes sex, exercise, sleep, and adornment that makes you feel creative and productive.

6. Set an intention to ignite eros each day. "Today at work, it is my intention to seek and find passionate love in everything I do. Today, I embody passionate love."

7. In your practice of stillness, open your heart to God's passion, satisfaction, and fulfillment.

8. Write a love letter to your work.

9. Place photos of the people you love in your work space.

10. Envision feeling completely and totally satisfied after completing a project or work task. What just happened? What does it feel like?

This Week's To-Be List

11

Be Clear

Simply let your "Yes" be "Yes,"
and your "No," "No."

MATTHEW 5:37

Julietta is a winner. A powerful woman, she earned a degree in finance and worked her way up to the corner office in a brokerage firm. She comfortably lopes ahead of a pack of men in her profession. She's earned their respect because she has a knack for leveraging relationships to get her clients to sign the bottom line.

But lately, Julietta has been struggling at work. She is chronically tired, mostly because her bouts of anxiety make sleep difficult. To compensate, she comes into work on the weekends, even though her boss never asked her to. She believes she will be less stressed on Monday if she can catch up ahead of time. Julietta tells herself, *It's just part of the deal.*

Julietta likes feeling competent. She likes the adrenaline rush of making her quarterly goals. She likes hanging out in her office. Her anxiety is quite an odd feeling—something unexpected. She's never been an anxious person, and none of her coworkers seem anxious. So where is it coming from?

Boundaries Prevent Burnout

Julietta's yes, while seemingly working out well for her, actually isn't working for her at all. She engages hard; she's all-in. That's how she's gotten ahead, and she's proud of it. But now her energy is consumed by the anxiety she feels. She doesn't know how to get back her fire, her eros. Set boundaries? No way. That would hold Julietta back.

Or would it?

Jesus had wise words about boundaries. In Matthew 5:33-37, Jesus is teaching the crowd about all kinds of life strategies—how to deal with anger and lust, for example. He then teaches them a different way of looking at commitments:

> Again, you have heard that it was said to the people long ago, "Do not break your oath, but fulfill to the Lord the vows you have made." But I tell you, do not swear an oath at all: either by heaven, for it is God's throne; or by the earth, for it is his footstool; or by Jerusalem, for it is the city of the Great King. And do not swear by your head, for you cannot make even one hair white or black. All you need to say is simply "Yes" or "No"; anything beyond this comes from the evil one.

In this statement, Jesus is issuing a radical challenge to rethink how and why we make commitments. There is a power dynamic when you make a commitment. When you say yes, the person or organization trusts you to follow through. They rely on you to deliver the product, time, or investment that's been promised.

The power is then totally in your hands. Will you come through, or won't you? That's a powerful position to be in. It means that a person or a group needs you. Or likes you. Admires or respects you and definitely relies on you. This interpersonal dynamic does something counter to the heart of Divine Love: It feeds the ego.

When you say yes in order to feed your ego, you manipulate others, even if you are not aware of it. This is a misuse of power, and it creates confusion and distrust. Jesus is pointing this out and asking us to think about doing it in a different way.

I don't believe Jesus is telling us to avoid making commitments. Instead, I think he's asking us to live a life of simplicity. A life of trusting that God knows the future. A life that moves you toward strengthening your relationships. This requires knowing yourself and your situation, including your limitations. Then you can say yes or no...and mean it.

When you choose to live your life in this way, your yes or no comes from a place of authenticity. It pours love and respect into the world.

Did you ever consider the fact that saying no might show *more* respect than less? That's what it meant in Julietta's life. Here's what she had to say: "During the time in my life when I didn't have boundaries, I had an internal, unexpressed anger and resentment. When I got in touch with my inner voice and become clearer with myself, I felt less stuck. By learning to set boundaries, I created more room for healthier relationships."

Setting Boundaries Shows Respect for Yourself

Saying yes when you really mean "no," "maybe," or "wait" leads to anger, resentment, and bitterness. You've made a commitment that you never wanted to make, can't keep, or can keep only with great effort (and possibly to the detriment of other commitments). You honor yourself when you acknowledge what you truly want and what you can truly do.

Setting Boundaries Shows Respect for Others

Environments with poor boundaries can feel like a culture of chaos. People often fear boundaries because they believe they will create relational distress. But in fact, boundaries create healthier relationships because they increase safety and trust. You know exactly what to expect both from yourself and others.

Have you ever been in a relationship where you emotionally needed something from the other person? We all have. Mutual emotional support is a foundation of relationship, and it's part of God's design. But when you enter a relationship with the sole purpose of meeting your own needs...well, that's an act of the ego again. It's probably not your intention, but it happens.

Instead, respectful relationships are built on mutual support, which means seeing the other person and striving to meet their needs. When two people start from a place of wholeness, the relationship thrives from a healthy balance of power. It's peaceful and respectful rather than filled with drama.

Respect for yourself and others is awesome burnout prevention because it helps you control how and where you spend your time. You are able to participate in activities and projects that replenish your energy and joy. You are able to clearly communicate your needs to your boss and colleagues. And it just feels awesome to know who you are, live authentically with no apologies, and communicate your needs clearly.

Poor boundaries lead to a culture of chaos.

It takes intentionality to create boundaries and follow up with action. When you make this intentional decision, you will experience a shift in your perspective, and your heart will soon follow. It will become easier to slow down, simplify your life, and say yes or no like you mean it.

The Rush

When Julietta took the time to be still, she realized a few important things. First, she became aware that she loved being known as a high performer. It gave her an adrenaline rush to close a big deal. Ending the day at happy hour while sharing high-fives with the guys felt so gratifying, and she appreciated the accolades from her sales manager too. Second, she realized that by working hard all the time, she spent less time at home. As a single person and an empty nester, she felt bored and lonely at home.

It wasn't until she began having panic attacks that she knew she needed to do something different. She decided to listen to her anxiety instead of fight it. What was God trying to teach her through the panic attacks?

Women and Men

How do you set boundaries in your work/career? It seems like the workplace is all about boundaries, but they are usually called something else. Policies and procedural manual, anyone?

Since the 1940s, women have been an integral part of the workforce. However, the work environment continues to be affected by cultural expectations of how women should behave. This can provoke some uncertainty about boundaries. How can I be assertive without being labeled as aggressive? How friendly should I be with my male coworkers? If I'm too friendly, perhaps it will be taken the wrong way...

For men, setting boundaries often comes naturally. Men are guided by a truth-and-justice orientation, which makes it easier to say yes or no despite how others may feel. Their challenge is to set boundaries in ways that create bridges rather than a divide. Men may benefit from practicing compassionate communication styles. (Learning compassionate communication benefits women too!)

In setting boundaries, a wise strategy for both women and men is consistency. Determine what boundaries are necessary for your work setting in order to perform your job at your best and to respect people. Live out those boundaries in every interaction. This approach will help you make decisions quickly and reduce confusion in your interactions.

As Julietta practiced being still, she realized that her adrenaline throughout the day kept her going in a challenging environment. "Bouncing from place to place, deal to deal...I fed off that energy. It was almost like an addiction." The adrenaline also created a buffer for her fear and pain of being alone. As soon as Julietta realized these things, she made a decision to heal.

"I realized that my boss never asked me to work weekends and that by working weekends I was not being truthful with my boss about what it really took to get the job done. As soon as I started saying no and choosing healthier patterns, I had more respect for myself. I was still productive, but I let go of the internal pressure to perform. If I met my goals, great—if I didn't, then it was because the workload was too high and not because of a failure on my part."

Can you identify with any parts of Julietta's story? If you were to be still and listen to what your pain, stress, or fear is trying to tell you, what would it say?

Be Clear with Others

Does setting boundaries come easy? Not at all...otherwise, I wouldn't be writing a chapter about it! If you have a hard time with boundaries, have no fear. Here are three simple aspects to focus on and language you can use to incorporate them.

Boundary #1: Self-Care

Caring for yourself has to happen first; otherwise, you can't take care of anything, especially work or your family. Get out your day planner right now and fill in your self-care time for the month. Yes, I'm serious! If you like color coordinating, grab a few different colors of Sharpies and go for it. Are you ready? Schedule these items for the next four weeks:

- 15 to 20 minutes a day for spiritual time
- 30 minutes a day to move and sweat

- 90 minutes a day to prepare and eat healthy food in a calm environment with people you enjoy
- 7 to 9 hours a day of rest, including naps
- all the important events related to your family, including holidays and special events
- one date night a week with your sweetie (If you don't have a sweetie, schedule one fun evening out with friends.)
- one 24-hour Sabbath a week
- one weekend away a month
- 2 to 4 weeks of vacation a year. No cell phone (except for emergencies). No laptop. Beach novels only. (Well, this book is allowed!)

What happens if you are asked to do a work project or hold a meeting during your self-care time? Say, "I'm sorry, I have another appointment at that time. Let's find a different time." You *do* have an appointment. A very important one—with yourself.

Boundary #2: Work

Even though you are an employee paid to complete a task, it's okay to set boundaries. Your boss doesn't own you; you are paid to complete a specific set of tasks within a specific time frame. (This holds true even if you are an entrepreneur and are your own boss. In that case, it's even more important to set boundaries!)

- Know exactly what your job description says. If you are asked to do more, set a boundary. "I would love to consider that project, but that's currently out of the scope of my job duties. Can we have a conversation about extra compensation, a title change, or a promotion before I consider saying yes?"
- Create an outline of what you want to achieve for the day, week, month, quarter, and year. Consider what is realistic

to achieve. It's easy to overestimate what you can accomplish, so for one week, keep very good notes on the time you spend on tasks. Consider downloading a time tracker app on your phone or tablet to get an accurate estimate. Once you have a realistic idea of the time needed, then you can easily outline your goals.

Having realistic goals written helps you relax about navigating your workday. It also helps you clearly communicate with your boss about what you can realistically achieve. The boundary? Accomplish your goals first before taking on any more projects. "I'd love to consider that assignment, but I am focused on achieving [insert goal] this week. Let's talk about that once I'm finished."

- Set aside 30 minutes each Friday afternoon to plan your goals for the next week. Write your weekly goals into an appointment on your calendar for eight o'clock Monday morning (or whenever your work week starts). When you begin the week, open that appointment and review your goals. Pray about them and ask for God's help.

- Do the hardest tasks during the time of day when you have the most mental clarity. I call this time your "power hours." Doing the most difficult work, or work that requires the most focus, during your power hours saves you a lot of frustration. It also cuts down the time it takes you to complete the more difficult tasks.

What does it mean if it's difficult for you to set boundaries around work? If you gain a strong sense of identity from work or experience a deep responsibility for work, you may have a harder time setting boundaries. Start small if this is true for you. Choose one of the suggestions above and implement it until you feel comfortable to do more. See how this one shift can change things for you over time.

Boundary #3: Personal Relationships

The big question here is, does this relationship drain my energy or restore it? Set boundaries to ensure that your energy is restored. For example, do you have difficult or even toxic coworkers? Unfortunately, your coworkers may not share your work ethic, or they may want to talk about their personal lives too much at work. It's totally okay to set boundaries with them.

Shift your perspective to view your coworkers as members of a team, not necessarily people you should hang out with in your free time. It is important to be kind and friendly to your coworkers, but if they drain your energy, you don't have to have any relationship with them other than a professional one. "Thank you for the invitation to grab a bite after work today, but I have another commitment that I need to attend to."

Finding the ever-precarious balance in work and family is a challenge! I mentioned a few lines ago to schedule all your important child and family events as part of your self-care. Doing so psychologically reinforces your family as your first priority. It also ensures that you will have enough energy to attend and participate in family events. However, I encourage you to think about family events on a stepwise priority basis. Do you have to attend every single event? It can be helpful to designate some events as "can't miss" and "could miss." This allows you the flexibility to choose whether to attend if you are tired or have a deadline at work.

Finally—and this the hardest one—spend some time thinking about your personal relationships. Ideally, your deepest relationships should refresh your energy through mutual support and encouragement. If they don't, something needs to change, even if it means that you limit these relationships. Yes, you can make decisions about who you spend your time with. It's not un-Christian to let a relationship go or set boundaries if that relationship is not healthy or doesn't bring the oneness that God desires. You don't have to cut off people in a spirit of

anger or indifference. Just focus your energy in relationships that ultimately return that same energy to you.

Spend a few moments now thinking about your personal relationships. Who in your life restores your energy? How can you invest in
that relationship? Who in your life sucks your energy dry? How can
you set limits? Again, it doesn't mean that you cut them off—frankly,
you can't cut off all the difficult people in your life (especially family!).
But you can limit your time with them and ensure that you have sched-
uled self-care time immediately afterward in order to replenish your
energy reservoir.

It's all about intention. Boundaries ensure that you carefully think
through who you are and what you need, and then respectfully insist
on meeting your needs (both alone and with others). Boundaries help
you know where you end and others begin. You may have a lot of
empathy for others, but you don't have to feel responsible for things
that aren't yours.

It's also okay to have different boundaries for different settings. For
example, you can limit personal information in the workplace and
save it for your intimate relationships. Navigate
these boundary roles by clearly understanding
the context of your relationships at work. Don't
allow yourself to step over a boundary. If you
do by accident, do the repair work you need to
bring stability to yourself and your work team
again.

> You don't
> have to feel
> responsible
> for things that
> are not yours.

Like Julietta, have you ever felt that setting
boundaries would be a detriment rather than a benefit to your work?
Actually, the opposite is true—having boundaries fosters your love for
your career. You know exactly who you are and what you can give, and
you work in that authenticity. Instead of expending so much of yourself

that all your passion burns out quickly, you are able to give and receive energy in balance. You are restored when you say no to something that drains all your energy. You are ignited when you say yes to something that fuels your creativity.

Let your yes be yes, and your no, no...and fall in love again.

Can You Have Too Many Boundaries?

Have you ever met someone who seemed rigid and inflexible? Sometimes boundaries can be set too forcefully, to the detriment of the work environment. These are not boundaries; they are walls. These types of people lack empathy and kindness toward others, and they can be very difficult to work with.

Yes, you can have too many boundaries or boundaries that work against you rather than for you. As with any other interpersonal skill, setting boundaries should always be in the spirit of moving toward relationship instead of away from it. Before you set a boundary, ask yourself these questions:

- What boundary will keep me healthy?
- What boundary will keep the other person, the relationship, or the organization healthy?
- How can I communicate this boundary in a respectful and loving way?
- What evidence do I need to modify or retract my boundary?

Boundaries can and should be updated depending on changes, context, interpersonal needs, and a variety of other factors. Seek God's leading; you will know you are on the right track when you feel his peace.

Chapter 11 Key Points

- Boundaries come from a place of personal authenticity.
- Learn simple strategies to be clear with others.
- Boundaries should always further relationship, not detract from it.

Practice Being Clear

Be still before God. Remove any distractions that may be present. Sit or lie comfortably, close your eyes, and open your hands. Pray or meditate:

God, I often feel like saying yes when I should say no. I understand that saying yes too much is unhealthy for me, for my relationships, and for others. Teach me healthy boundaries at work. Give me the strength to say no when I need to.

This Week's To-Be List

_____

_____

_____

_____

_____

_____

_____

_____

_____

_____

_____

_____

_____

_____

_____

_____

_____

_____

12

Be Whole

You created my inmost being; you knit
me together in my mother's womb.

PSALM 139:13

t's the morning rush at Starbucks, and the line extends way out the
door. You're an accident waiting to happen if you don't get your coffee soon. So. Very. Grumpy. But you *have* to down your quad shot
to function, which means you have to wait if you want to be human
today. Ten minutes late for work already, and you notice a voicemail
from the school. Great. One of your kids forgot their permission slip
for a field trip. Which means you are going to be even later.

Why is everything...just...so...loud? Your senses are heightened by
the *dinky-doink* of the crosswalk and the exhaust of the cars zooming
through the yellow lights. The man reading a newspaper over there
would be so much more handsome if his tie wasn't that irritating paisley,
and you cannot believe how that yoga-pants mama dragging a screaming toddler away from the counter cookies just spoke to her boyfriend
on the cell phone. Outside, a bike courier blitzes through a group

of punk teens who think it's hilarious to stay in his way. The courier swears and the punks flip him off, and everything just keeps on moving.

Oh yeah. It's gonna be a great day.

Finally, your coffee. Caffeine to jolt you through your back-to-backs. Why is the daily grind peppered with such chaos? You take a sip. And then another. Your headache begins to dissipate, and your energy rises. Well, maybe it's not all that chaotic. You just have to figure out how to get your stuff together, and then everything will be okay.

God's Analeptic

Your days are, well, hard. Have we really, truly acknowledged that yet? They are. Your life is hard. You need your coffee, and you deserve it too. Love-energy for work? It takes a lot to remember that heat. Your work is like a long-term relationship that has seen better days. In the beginning, you and your work were so tight, but after many seasons of quad-shot espressos just getting you through, the strings binding your passion have worn threadbare.

That's the hardest thing to swallow.

At my workplace, we have a hard time keeping our stuff together too. Then it morphs into the never-ending focal point on balance. At the start of each academic quarter, my colleagues and I have a conversation that goes like this:

"What are your goals for the quarter?"

"Balance." We all smile and nod our heads in agreement. "And how about yours?"

"Umm, well, I want to do good self-care and get everything done."

Of course, we have no idea what balance really means because at the end of the quarter, we are haggard, dragging ourselves back to the drawing board and muttering about doing things different next quarter. Clearly, we have some work to do, in a very paradoxical way.

During these conversations, I envision Philippe Petit on August 6, 1974, walking the cable strung between the two former World Trade Center towers. The daredevil stunt was illegal, of course, and he and his friends planned an elaborate scheme to make it happen, fully knowing that Philippe was taking the ultimate risk with his life. Yet he seemed so smug and sure about it. The people on the street below were stunned to see a figure a quarter-mile above them, seemingly walking on air. And he succeeded! Now *that's* balance.

Because if we're being really honest, many of us feel more like a tightrope walker who falls off the cable, splatting ourselves into gridlock. You never read about the ones that fall off the wire because...they died. They failed at balance. You yourself might be thinking, *Balance? Show me how, and I'll be just as shocked as all those New Yorkers.*

Let's get even more honest: Most of us stink at balance. If you didn't, you wouldn't be reading this book. You wouldn't be burned out, and you'd be scheming up wilder adventures than Mr. Petit. I wouldn't have been a crispy-fried social worker at age 25, trying to figure out how to manage *all the things*...and I didn't even have kids then. Now in my midforties, I'm realizing the balance convos didn't land well because I kept chugging through five more years of graduate school, a dissertation, two books, and fervent prayers that my clients didn't hurt anyone with either the fifth of Jack Daniels or the rifle they kept in their pickup trucks. (I've encountered some pretty interesting situations in my work—makes *Jersey Shore* look like Disneyland.)

I fought an internal war about writing this chapter. On one hand, I know how important this topic is. The research is pretty clear that an out-of-control environment fuels your burnout like a snag in a lightning storm fuels a fire. On the other hand, I'm not the poster girl for balance. I love to work, and I work a lot. I also feel compelled to work, even when I need to rest. It's like the U2 song: "Work, I can't live with or without you." Some days it's like borderline personality disorder on a quad-shot espresso.

Jesus, please send some relief! (I mean that literally.)

Thankfully, Jesus saves. He's always got a plan B to hustle you and me through our busy lives. Since we are on the honesty train, I had to take some time to remind myself exactly what that is. This morning, after stillness and several cups of coffee, God sang his analeptic over me:

> When peace like a river, attendeth my way,
> When sorrows like sea billows roll
> Whatever my lot, thou hast taught me to know
> It is well, it is well with my soul.
> —HORATIO GATES SPAFFORD

Ah, peace. My old friend, how I have missed you! It's been a while. I didn't recognize you the other day, standing beside me at Starbucks.

The root of the word "peace" comes from the Greek verb *eírō*, which means "to tie, join, fasten, or string together." Interestingly, *eírō* is also the same verb that eros (passionate love) is derived from. Peace is mistakenly believed to be a feeling or state of mind, but that is the manifestation of it (*eirēnē*) and not the root (*eírō*). In the New Testament, Jewish and Greek writers used one word for peace—*eirēnē*—referring to a state of rest. However, *eirēnē* is not the fullness of *eírō*—rather, it is a derivative of it.

Rest and Reconnect

Isaiah 9:6 describes the Messiah as the Prince of Peace. Jesus is both the model and the embodiment of wholeness. Understanding the deeper meaning of the word "peace" can radically reframe your understanding of his mission. Jesus (wholeness) intentionally moved toward humanity to redeem us in our state of unrest (fear, pain, abandonment). God's plan is for you to experience wholeness because it is the answer to your stress and pain...and burnout too.

Take a few minutes to meditate on this idea. How can you move toward wholeness at work today?

"Peace" is much more a verb than a noun. At its root, peace requires intentional movement toward unity (with others) and oneness (with God and yourself). The resulting state begets wholeness. When you are whole, and when you have joined with others in wholeness, you experience the fullness of *eírō*—stability and harmony.

> Peace is an intentional process that leads to wholeness.

Peace (*eírō*) is the same love-energy of God that you learned about in chapter 10. It just gets you to a different place than eros. Which is probably a good thing. To get through that line at Starbucks, you are going to need a little more *eirēnē* than eros.

Peace or in Pieces?

You may have thought I made a mistake in Spafford's hymn back there, but actually, I wrote it in his original words. Spafford's four-year-old son had died of scarlet fever. Two years later, his wife and daughters were crossing the Atlantic when their ship was struck by another vessel, killing 226 people, including all four of Spafford's daughters. He wrote his iconic song while sailing to England to meet his wife in Europe.

When I was a kid, I learned that third line as "thou hast taught me to *say*," not "thou hast taught me to *know*." Did you learn it that way too? When I realized I had been singing it wrong my whole life, I was a little peeved. Not only does the word "know" rhyme better, but I think that's probably the word Spafford wanted all along.

Knowing is much different from saying. Knowing is how you know what you know without seeing, hearing, or learning it. It's not a feeling, and it's not a thought. It comes from the soul. Some describe it as intuition; others describe it as the Holy Spirit. I think of it as God's love-energy guiding you toward his highest good.

Knowing is the reason that, like Mr. Spafford, you can sail past the spot where tragedy occurred and still declare your faith. It's the reason you can be like Mr. Petit on a cable strung between two skyscrapers with 65 mph wind gusts and chuckle in delight. Since your knowing led you there, you deeply trust that you will be okay. In fact, you don't even question whether you will be okay, or ask anyone if you will be okay, or need to talk through being okay; you just *know you will be okay*. You have a deep sense of security that goes beyond words.

That's peace.

Knowing leads to peace. Peace knits you together in wholeness.

Wholeness means all your broken pieces are bound back together. Dissonance dissolves. There's no war within yourself; there's no war with others. There's no need for war because all the parts of your being—heart, body, mind, soul—are lovingly attended to. You stop resisting the hard things—fear, pain, trauma, grief...things you cannot control—and accept them as a part of the whole life God gave you. It's the balanced life described in Ecclesiastes 7:14: "When times are good, be happy; but when times are bad, consider this: God has made the one as well as the other."

Since knowing comes from the great I AM, the holder of the universe, you *know* you will be okay.

I think Spafford was referring to this kind of knowing. Though his grief was deep, he would still be whole. This knowing kept him through the dark night of his soul. Held by peace, he wasn't split into pieces by his circumstances.

In your work, have you changed up the words? Have you made it about what you say or do—or even what you think or feel—and turned away from your knowing?

Has it left you in pieces?

No wonder burnout has robbed you; the door of your soul was unlocked. When you are in pieces, what you do, say, think, and feel comes from a state of unrest; it comes from fear. But when you are whole, you live and breathe and move in a state of authenticity, which then informs everything you do, say, think, and feel. You embody the truest version of yourself, a marvelous soul sparked from the Divine.

Women and Men

Is it possible to achieve wholeness in your work and career? It's different for women and men.

Women need to perceive they are loved in order to feel whole. However, it can be a challenge to find appropriate ways to show love in the workplace. One easy way is to search for the best in a woman's work. Can you highlight something she's said or done that reflects her best? Compliment her on what you noticed. "You worked so hard on that deal. Even though it fell through, I noticed how important it was for you to take care of your clients. That's inspiring to me."

To feel whole, men need to perceive that they are trusted. Men automatically feel devotion from those who depend on them. Expressed devotion is a way to help a man feel respected. Again, it can be a challenge to show respect appropriately in the workplace. One way is to verbally endorse a man when he is leading a project or team. "We believe in you. We trust your leadership." It's a simple statement, yet it will radically encourage him.

Another nice effect of living authentically is that you become a rock star at work! Love flows freely and naturally because you do not fear what others do to you, say about you, think about you, or feel about you. "There is no fear in love. But perfect love drives out fear, because fear has to do with punishment. The one who fears is not made perfect in love" (1 John 4:18). You can feel passion at work—and for work—once again simply by allowing God to reknit you in peace.

Reknitting Your Pieces

I want the whole thing, Amy. But the pieces of my life are just...so much.
"Peace, dude!" Easy to say, but not easy to achieve. The culture—the

entire universe—aches for peace. But with one click of the remote, we can clearly see that humanity is unraveled. Developing peace comes through intentional, regular action. But therein

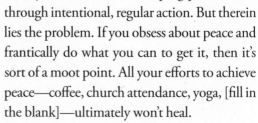

Instead of attempting to achieve peace, work toward establishing wholeness.

lies the problem. If you obsess about peace and frantically do what you can to get it, then it's sort of a moot point. All your efforts to achieve peace—coffee, church attendance, yoga, [fill in the blank]—ultimately won't heal.

Psalm 139:13-14 is such a beautiful metaphor of God's desire for your wholeness. Even as you developed in your mother's womb, God knit all of you together—all your pieces and parts—into your core personhood.

> You created my inmost being;
>   you knit me together in my mother's womb.
> I praise you because I am fearfully and wonderfully made;
>   your works are wonderful, I know that full well.

How amazing! Even more amazing, this verse shows the way to develop peace. Instead of, "How do I achieve peace?" the better question to ask is, "How do I achieve wholeness?"

Wholeness is the fulfillment of peace. It comes simply by knitting your unraveled pieces back together with God's help. Read this next section slowly, and take some time to reflect on your unraveled pieces. Can you identify with any of the stories? Is God showing you how he wants to knit your pieces back together?

Pieces Within Yourself

Blair has a shopping addiction. Well, it's not *really* an addiction if it's not a problem, right? She makes plenty of money and isn't in debt. But her closets are crammed full of stuff, and she owns properties, cars, and an RV she never uses. She works hard, and shopping makes her feel better. She's proud of what she's earned—or so she thinks. She's caught in a cycle of impulse shopping, satisfying the impulse, and then repeating the same pattern a few days later. She feels satisfied and happy after a purchase, but she never feels true peace.

What is in pieces in Blair's life? What has been split off from her truest self? After stillness and reflection, Blair realizes that she has split off her need to be nurtured. She expends a lot of energy attending to her job and family, and it's not returned. Even deeper, she's the one who's gotten in the way of receiving nurture because she projects a persona of independence. If Blair would allow God to nurture her and to teach her to receive nurture from others, things might really change.

Rest and reflect: What pieces within yourself have been split off by your work? How does God want to knit them back together?

Pieces with Others

Damon is an isolated man. He's never really felt understood. Never a husband or father, he struggles to believe that love is real. As a result, he's always preferred working swing shifts. He's stoic and strong, and the rest of the world isn't. The less interaction with people, the better.

One night, Damon stops at a bar to grab a beer after work. Some guys ask him to play pool, and he does. The next night he does the same thing, as well as the night after that. Months later, Damon drinks too much and gets a DUI on his way home. A judge mandates that he undergo a treatment program to avoid losing his driver's license. Damon's job requires a valid driver's license, so he hesitantly agrees to the treatment. But he's afraid. Playing pool with the guys at the bar is one thing, but group therapy—sharing his feelings with a bunch of strangers—that is quite another.

What is in pieces in Damon's life? How has he been split off from others? Damon's self-defeating thoughts have forged thick barriers in his relationships. Yet the way the culture has isolated him is also part of the problem. In both metaphorical and physical ways, Damon hides himself. After reflection, Damon realized that he has split off his need for connection. His loneliness prompted him to say yes to hanging out with the guys at the bar, which actually was a great step toward wholeness. But saying yes to too many drinks split him off again. If Damon would allow God to teach him how to engage in relationships that were fun as well as had limits, his life would radically change.

Rest and reflect: What pieces with others have been split off by your work? How does God want to knit them back together? How might God be asking you to reach out to others who feel split into pieces?

Pieces with the Greater Whole

As I write this section, I am reminded of the world's current issues, such as the climate, immigration, and nationalism. Regardless of where you stand on these and other issues, they affect your well-being. They also influence your relationships with others.

Peace includes engaging in intentional processes to bind things back together. Peace also includes holding God's creation in awe and actively engaging in the stewardship of the natural world. In the greater whole, this means actively bringing people together to coexist in harmony. As Christians share agape—the highest form of Divine love—we take one more step toward each other. We don't just coexist, we actively love others, including those we perceive to be enemies. We are open to understanding our own privilege. We act to remedy injustice and sustain our environment even when we don't perceive that those issues affect us directly.

Rest and reflect: What pieces of the greater whole have been split off by your work? How does God want to knit them back together? How might God be leading you to engage in peace-making with the greater whole?

———— ∞ ————

Peace is not something you find. It's not something you achieve. It's something you develop. Like fulfillment, it's something you cultivate.

The higher ethic of peace is to live with authenticity, which comes from wholeness. This principle is life-giving and empowers you to walk in your calling. Chapters 13 and 14 will spark more thought about living authentically as a called, whole person.

Like everything with God, the bottom line of wholeness is to exist in genuine relationship. When you are whole—embodying your true self—and those with whom you are in relationship are whole as well, *wow*! That's powerful, transformative, and healing relationship.

Wholeness enables you to live with authenticity.

Peace is still about love and oneness, but it's a state of rest instead of passion. In your work and in your life, passion and rest must synchronize in balance. Too much rest and you'd never get anything done. Too much passion and...well, you can probably guess where that would get you!

Isn't it amazing, though, that rest and passion lead you to the same place? *Eírō*. Oneness. That's God. That's the kind of relationship he wants with you. It's the kind of relationship he envisions for your work and with those you love. It's what you are designed for, and what your heart longs for. Through his passion and grace, let him knit your unraveled pieces back together.

It Is Well

In the final stages of writing this book, I left this chapter for last. I'm not sure how that happened. In the compilation of research, conversations about content, and decisions about flow, I revised chapter 12 many times. I think it had four different titles and foci before it settled into "Be Whole."

No denying it—I was frustrated with this chapter. I felt like I was dealing with a child who refuses to tie their shoes and get in the car when you are late for work. With severe writer's block and a looming deadline, I found my sleep severely compromised. I was waking up at two, three, and four a.m., letters and words spinning in my frenzied mind. If you had seen me during the last few writing weeks, my puffy eyes and slow-moving pace would have pinged all your nurturing heartstrings. *Amy, you look so tired! Get that book done!*

You probably noticed my satirical tone at the beginning of this chapter. Sarcasm and cynicism are signals that I am exhausted and overwhelmed. No shocker here—I was the one at Starbucks standing in tenuous fragility. But caffeine only does so much; I needed something stronger. The only thing I knew to do—well, actually, the only thing I *could* do—was be still, because everything else I tried just wasn't working.

In stillness, I began to realize that my early morning waking was not anxiety or stress. Rather, it was the love-energy of God writing the words of this book. It was his *eírō* for you and me that he wanted me to transcribe. When I finally understood—when I finally *knew* what all the tension was about—I honored it. I rose in eros when God woke me, and I wrote. I sat in *eirēnē* when he asked me to, and I wrote.

My tangential, frenetic rant melted into a song. I felt whole, grounded, and secure, with a deep trust that my typing fingers were actually footsteps on the path God beckoned me to walk. Despite the fact that I was physically tired with much left to do, my energy was restored. Soon after, chapter 12 was born.

In chapter 5, we discussed how rest is a necessity for healing burnout. Through the process of writing this book, I have come to realize that there are two kinds of rest. There is the kind of rest that restores your body and mind—such as sleep, a fun hobby, or a vacation. But there is another kind of rest that is deeper, that binds together all your fragmented parts. This rest comes from listening to your *knowing*. It comes from hearing the call of your soul and honoring it.

Peace through the storm.

Confidence on the cable.

Equanimity at Starbucks.

May you know. May it be well with your soul.

Chapter 12 Key Points

- Peace (*eirēnē*) is the same love-energy of God (*eirō*, oneness) as passionate love (eros).
- Peace is an intentional process that leads to wholeness.
- True rest comes from listening to what you know.

Practice Being Whole

Spend some time with God. Remove any distractions that may be present. Sit or lie comfortably, close your eyes, and open your hands. Pray or meditate:

God, my exhausted heart is split into pieces. Sometimes I even feel permanently broken. Help me intentionally move toward wholeness. Bind me together in your supernatural peace.

This Week's To-Be List

13

Be Retooled

His master replied, "Well done, good and faithful servant! You have been faithful with a few things; I will put you in charge of many things."

MATTHEW 25:21

Donna was a go-getter her whole life. A dedicated Christian wife and mother, she raised four girls and a garden larger than your imagination. Her summer tomatoes alone provided salsa, salads, and sauce for the entire neighborhood! When her daughters left home and had kids of their own, Donna and her husband became foster parents to boys in the juvenile system. It was their calling and a way to give back. They loved the Lord and they loved people, and they shared that love with everyone they encountered.

But it wasn't enough. In her midfifties, Donna went back into the workforce as an administrative assistant at a university. She quickly learned that one of the perks of her job was a tuition discount, so Donna wasted no time in pursuing her baccalaureate degree. She commuted 20 miles to work every day on icy highways in the winter, worked full-time, and studied—all while fulfilling her service calling from the Lord.

A few years later, she graduated as a distinguished student in her program, which was quite an honor. Earning her degree increased her salary and respect among her colleagues. Donna was just like that servant in Matthew 25:21—a faithful woman who proved herself and was gradually entrusted with more. But it didn't all come overnight. What did it take to get her there?

You Are Talented!

I love Jesus's parable in Matthew 25:14-28. This is the story of the master who had three servants and left them with bags of gold—five bags, two bags, and one bag, respectively—before going on a long journey. The servants with five bags and two bags immediately went out and found a way to double them. When the master returned, these servants proudly presented their ten and four bags back to their master. The master, thoroughly pleased, honored them and rewarded them with more responsibility. But the servant with one bag of gold had buried it. When the master returned, that servant had only the one bag to give back. The master called him wicked and lazy, took away his bag of gold, and threw him out.

That reaction sounds kind of harsh, doesn't it? The whole concept of the servant-master thing weirds me out anyway because that kind of power differential isn't appropriate or relevant. But let's look at the deeper meaning of the story because there's a major takeaway if you are thinking about retooling.

What is retooling? If you work in manufacturing, you know this term well! Retooling is getting a new set of machinery to do a job better or to do a different job altogether. The goal is to improve. Retooling helps you to advance or to do work that's different from what you are doing now. It's necessary when you make a job or career change and can include improving your skill set through new education, training, or experience.

You might consider retooling if you are burned out and don't see an option for resolving your burnout in your current job or career. In fact, you may have dreamed of doing something else for a long time! If you are just trying to make it work at work but know deep down that you can't, then perhaps it's time to think about different options.

> The goal of retooling is vocational improvement and increased job satisfaction.

In my years of career counseling, I've observed that the decision to retool is one of the scariest. Retooling midcareer poses challenges that weren't present when you began your career. You usually have more bills to pay, and you likely have family issues like childcare, custody arrangements, extended family needs, and transportation. You could be paying down student loans from your first or second training program. Would going back to school actually be worth the cost?

The decision can be overwhelming and frightening, but you know you can't stay where you are. Your burnout is too great, and you're not going to last much longer. But you don't know where to start. The very first step?

Accept that your work isn't working for you anymore, *and that's okay*. It's normal for things to change over the years. It's normal for you to want to grow. It's normal to get bored, tired, and frustrated with coworkers. It's all normal. Allow yourself to feel what you feel right now so you can move somewhere new.

You probably know that in Matthew 25, the traditional rendering of "bags of gold" was "talents." A talent was a unit of money, but the principle applies to the kind of talents we talk about today.

Now imagine you are one of the three servants. Actually, you *are* that servant. God has given you many gifts and talents, and he's pleased when you use them. If in your stress, fear, and exhaustion you bury what he's given you, what good will your talent be? You might still have it, but that's all you'll ever have.

Rest and Reconnect

You have several options when considering a career move:

- *Sidestep.* Take on a job that doesn't require additional training. An environmental, managerial, or personnel change can make all the difference.
- *Step ahead.* Take advantage of a promotion or advancement. You'll probably have many opportunities to do this during your career.
- *Step back.* Return to a job with less responsibility or strenuous duties. Or quit. A step back can be helpful when medical or psychological issues arise, or it could be forced due to extenuating circumstances, such as relocation or a remediation plan. In this case, emotional support is helpful.
- *Stay still.* Stay in your current job or career. This may be your best option if the benefits outweigh the drawbacks. I refer to this decision as "the golden handcuffs." You will still feel stuck, but the benefits of the job might help you manage that feeling.
- *Leap.* Choose a different job or career altogether. This option usually requires retooling, with more training, education, or experience.

As you consider the various types of career moves, you might be thinking, *I've known for years what I need to do. But for whatever reason, I just can't do it yet.* I encourage you to be still and ask yourself, *What's stopping me? Is it possible that burnout itself might be my biggest barrier right now?*

I'm sure the first two servants had a lot of trepidation before investing their bags of gold. After all, that money was worth a lot (a talent is worth approximately $1.4 million in today's economy). Why would the servants risk losing their master's investment? Something motivated them to improve. Interestingly, that motivation was never about the money or the talent itself. It was a desire to please the master by making good use of what they had been given, by multiplying it.

God is pleased when you develop the gifts he has given you. He's that proud parent saying "Atta kid!" just for your trying. What would it be like for you to improve your job skills or career situation? Your vocational satisfaction and emotional health are worth well more than $1.4 million. If God is leading you to retool, you are worth the risk of investment.

How to Retool

If your love-energy for work is absolutely gone and you know that there is no chance you will get it back (either at your current job or in your career), it's time to make a radical change. It's time to retool. This can feel a little ambiguous and even scary, but have no fear; using a step-by-step process will spark your confidence.

Step 1: Determine Whether Retooling Is Right for You

You have felt a desire to do something different, perhaps for quite a while. Many of my midlife counseling students feel this way. *I always wanted to be a counselor, but before I could pursue my dream, I had to be a parent* or *make more money* or *help with the family business.* In their earlier work years, they felt they had to do something different, but in midlife, things changed, allowing them to pursue their real career dream.

Is this how you feel too?

Envisioning a new career can be scary—and exhilarating. Seek God's wisdom and be led by the Holy Spirit. Do you remember our discussion on values and career satisfaction in chapter 10? Think about what you most value in work and how those values might inform your next career move. Allow them to play a significant role.

At this stage, the "how" is fairly ambiguous. *How am I going to support my family when I go back to school? How am I going to learn online when I don't know how to use a computer?* Right now, don't worry about the how. Focus on the what and where—what you want to do and where God is leading you. Have peace; if this is your calling and God's leading, he will make the how fall into place.

Step 2: Formulate a Plan

Please don't skip this step—it's so important! Gather all the information you need to formulate your career move. My best recommendation is to study labor market information, which are statistics compiled by the US government and free to the public. My favorite labor market website is the Occupational Information Network (O*NET) at https://www.onetonline.org. You can learn and peruse job duties, training requirements, salary information, and more about virtually any occupation you can think of. You can even learn about the values each occupation fulfills!

Another great way to collect information is through informational interviews. Talk to people working in professions that interest you. Visit them at their workplaces to get a feel for the work environments. People love to share about what they do, and a 30-minute interview is a worthwhile investment if you are considering spending thousands of dollars on an educational program.

Once you have collected all the information you can, create a plan to move forward. Use a calendar to create a timeline (start and end dates). Whip out your calculator to create a budget. If you need help with tuition and expenses, research about financial aid.

The most important item in your plan is a strong support system. Trust me, you are going to need it! Choose people who understand the demands of retooling—not only people who will empathize and be able to help you along the way but also those who will hold you accountable to reach your dream.

Step 3: Move Forward in Faith

The conflict between your logic and your heart can freeze you in place. Your head shouts all the reasons retooling might be a *really* bad idea, but your heart continues to softly whisper that you are on the right path. I can't possibly know what is right for you, but I want to encourage you to trust the Voice that gives you peace. You might struggle and face challenges, but when the Holy Spirit is leading, you will not fail.

Sometimes walking the path of peace *is* your calling. One of my former students, Chuck, had always dreamed of getting his PhD. I'll never forget the day he called and said that he had been accepted into a PhD program. But I heard ambivalence in his voice, and I knew something wasn't quite right. Within a month of beginning his program, he knew the timing was off, and he wasn't sure the program would open the doors he wanted. During our subsequent phone calls, we processed his next decision. Should he leap forward, stay still, or step back? Each option included many pros and cons. Ultimately, Chuck decided to quit the program because that decision gave him the most peace.

Move forward in faith.

When Chuck stepped back from the PhD program, he was actually moving forward in faith. Listen to the Voice that leads you and follow it, trusting that it's leading you to the place that's right for you.

Step 4: Use Your Support System

You are undoubtedly a self-sufficient, independent go-getter. That's the type of personality that thinks about vocational improvement...and also the type that is most likely to experience burnout. So this step is especially for you. Your support system is there for a reason: You need help along the way. You can't do this alone, especially if you have a lot of challenges to work through.

In step 2, you put together a support system of people who understand the demands of retooling. Reach out to them now for emotional, spiritual, and even financial support. It's also okay to ask for day-to-day help with things such as childcare, dog walking, transportation, and the like. They love you and want to share in your success, so let them be part of your team!

Another great thing that your support system can do? Talk you off a ledge when you want to quit. Because you are going to want to quit—I guarantee it. You will experience times of crisis or high anxiety when you retool. These times are exactly what your support system is there for. Again, it's so important to choose people who will actually be willing to hold you accountable to your dream and not give in when you want to give in.

Step 5: Celebrate

Ah, one of the most important parts of retooling!

Sometimes I have students who are so exhausted when they finish their program that they want to skip their commencement ceremony. When I see this, I give them yet one more lecture about how important it is to participate in their celebration. A celebration marks a rite of passage; you take a psychological and spiritual step forward when you commemorate what you have accomplished. It's also important for your support system to celebrate with you, because your achievement is their achievement too!

Women and Men

As women and men come closer to occupying the workforce equally, both genders face the retooling question. The same issues for retooling apply to both women and men—financial challenges, family needs, and overall stress load. Both women and men are typically motivated to retool to better the lives of their family and children, as well as to advance their careers or to improve their job satisfaction. If you love someone who is considering retooling (or are considering retooling yourself), use this opportunity to talk through it with your loved ones. You can grow together in your relationship if you believe that you are doing this together, for everyone's sake, rather than just for yourself.

Finally, be thinking about your next thing—your next goal. It's fine to rest and celebrate, but don't forget to open your heart to the next step the Holy Spirit has for you. Setting new goals—even small ones— keeps you looking toward the future. You stagnate when you live as if you have finished growing. Stagnation is part of burnout...something you want to avoid in the future!

When Talented Feels Selfish

I think one of the biggest reasons people feel anxious about retooling is the fear of being selfish. Depending on your circumstances, your retooling is likely to create some stress or changes for the people you love. (That's why they are in this with you too!) The fear of making your stress their stress can hold you back.

But what if your retooling was about a greater good? Consider Donna's reason: "My family and my faith helped me to reprioritize my life to continually honor a larger commitment. We have enough money; we accept this, and we don't need to be rich or strive for more. We can adjust our lives as necessary to find contentment because our family is clear on what is important to us—how we treat each other and those around us. We work hard to give back." For Donna, retooling was never selfish—it was about a greater good.

How can your retooling be about a greater good? Because when it is, it is never selfish. It's for them *and* for you.

It could be good for your family because it might lead to more financial provision. It could be good for your community because you serve as a credible volunteer or leader. It can be good for the global climate because you have more to give back. And it could be good for you because your burnout and health would improve, thus improving your relationships.

Are you are stuck in your burnout—stuck in an environment that will never change? Are you asking the environment to change around you, or are you ready to change yourself to fit the environment? Step out in faith and increase your talents.

A Five-Step Plan for Retooling

1. Determine if retooling is right for you.
2. Formulate a plan.
3. Move forward in faith.
4. Use your support system.
5. Celebrate when you've achieved your goal!

Work through each of these steps if you are considering retooling. Find a trusted source to help you, such as a career counselor or mentor. Practice being still, and open your heart to the leading of the Holy Spirit.

Moving on to Transcendence

Wow, we've covered a lot in the last four chapters! Now we're to the good part. The really, really good part—the fifth intention of burnout resolution.

Before you turn the page, I want to encourage you that *it is possible* to fall in love with work again. If you ever feel lost or unseen, as if no one loves you or identifies with your stress or burnout, remember what it is that made you: eros—passionate love from Love himself. It's the beckoning Lover from chapter 1. It's that Lover who wants to fulfill you completely and enable you to transcend. Your satisfaction is his satisfaction. You'll meet once again in chapters 14 and 15.

Chapter 13 Key Points

- God is pleased when you develop *all* the talents he gave you.
- You are allowed to retool; this is a natural process of growth throughout your vocational lifespan.
- Create a logistical and reasonable plan to retool.

Practice Being Retooled

Spend some time with the Holy Spirit. Remove any distractions that may be present. Sit or lie comfortably, close your eyes, and open your hands. Pray or meditate:

Holy Spirit, the ache of my heart about my work just won't quit. If my burnout won't resolve in my current situation, then please lead me with your wisdom and show me the path to retool.

This Week's To-Be List

The Five Intentions of Burnout Resolution

I.
I will practice stillness so God can
restore my soul.

II.
I will seek connection with God,
myself, and my work.

III.
I will cultivate awareness of who I am,
where I am, and what I want to be.

IV.
I will take consistent steps to
promote well-being in my work.

V.
**I will focus on who I am to *be*,
not what I am to *do*.**

14

Be Released

There is one body and one Spirit, just as you
were called to one hope when you were called.

EPHESIANS 4:4

The morning sun splashes its warmth on the mountains in front of you, illuminating their purple-pink grandeur. Despite last weekend's dusting of snow, late summer continues to hold its embrace of this perfect day. A lavender field stretches lazily before you, a welcome distraction from everything you need to get done today. You close your eyes and inhale its calm. The importance of your to-do list has faded, and there is nowhere else to look but up. It is a moment of perfect peace.

The clouds. They form so many shapes, so silently, so easily. Dancers effortlessly twirling and whirling and leaping across their sky-stage. They are simply there, open, gladly forming into the shapes and places the wind provides for them.

There appears to be no rhyme or reason to their dance. They are big and small; they billow and then disappear. They fill and release. They rain and relent. They are mysterious, worthy of awe and appreciation. They bless you with their beauty, and they seem to know it.

Have you ever contemplated the shifting clouds? They never appear the same way, ever. They are allowed to change because something bigger than them has created and placed them there. Their assignment is allowed to form just as they've been told to do.

Would you ever look at the changing clouds and think, *Those clouds aren't working hard enough to be appreciated by God*? You wouldn't because clouds are beautiful, no matter what their shape. More so, you have a deep understanding that God himself is shaping them. God's breath whispers them into being.

How then could you ever criticize what they become?

So it is with your calling. Like the clouds, your calling is formed by something bigger than you; it is formed by the breath of God. Your calling is fixed because, like the clouds, it exists. But it is fluid because God shapes it depending on the season and his purpose. Whatever your calling becomes, it is absolutely, amazingly, miraculously beautiful.

We've spent some wonderful moments together in these pages. Now that our time is almost over, we have one more important thing to do, which is to revisit your calling. In chapter 4, you learned that your vocational journey began with your calling; your calling was breathed into your heart by the Holy Spirit. You contemplated the concept of a lost calling and how to reconnect with it again. I hope you have been able to contemplate your calling throughout this book as you learned about where burnout comes from and how to heal from it.

Now I'd like to move one step further along the journey of realizing your calling. When you finish reading, I want you to put down this book and feel secure in your calling, both as it is now and as it might develop.

Did you ever take Psych 101—the class where you learned about the stages of human development? Humans change and develop as life progresses. What is important to you at age 16 is probably not important to you at age 36. What you need at age 29 is very different from what you need at age 54. Your natural changes are influenced by physiology, experience (including stress and crisis), maturation, and spiritual growth.

Your calling grows and develops just like the rest of you. Your passions and interests can become more or less fine-tuned, which is a natural result of growth. Sometimes God has new assignments for you. Those natural changes can raise existential or spiritual anxiety once again. How do you know whether you are walking in your calling? Let's consider the story of the prophet Jonah.

> **Vocational calling is both fixed and fluid.**
> ⸺⸙⸺

Rest and Reconnect

In chapter 4, you reflected on the calling that the Holy Spirit placed in your heart. Take a few moments to remember it now.

Has anything changed?

Consider that your calling can be both fixed and fluid. Right now, does your calling feel fixed or fluid? What feelings does this realization bring up for you?

What do you believe your next steps are in your vocational calling? Write, doodle, or draw whatever comes up for you.

It's About Who You Are

The Bible contains many Scriptures about vocational calling. But interestingly, very few of them give a specific assignment. Instead, they infer that calling is about relationships. For example...

Ephesians 4:4 calls us to unity and hope.

First Corinthians 1:9 calls us into fellowship with Jesus.

Second Timothy 1:9 calls us to live holy lives.

Our time together is too short to review all the biblical insights and stories on calling, but I encourage you to do your own study if you are interested. It can be a wonderful spiritual experience to increase your knowledge in this area, especially if you are contemplating your calling. The main point here is this: Just like most everything with God, calling is always about connection—it deepens your relationship with God and with others.

Let's look at Jonah's story. Jonah was an eighth-century BCE prophet sent by God to prophesy to the people of Nineveh about impending doom for their evil behaviors. God loved the people and wanted to save them, and he commissioned Jonah to warn them and encourage them to repent.

But as the story goes, Jonah was afraid because he believed the people would reject him and that his life ultimately would be in danger. He was also angry that God wanted to save the Ninevites; Jonah felt that they didn't deserve God's redemption. So he tried to escape his mission. What happened? He ended up in the belly of a great fish, only to be spit out, embarrassed, angry, and probably very stinky. Jonah eventually obeyed God, traveled to Nineveh, and preached the word of God's grace and love. The people repented and turned their hearts toward God.

It's a wonderful story—one that is often read to children and that you've probably heard many times yourself. It's a story of calling, because God clearly called Jonah to a task. But I would argue that going to Nineveh was not Jonah's calling. Jonah's *task*—his something to do—was to go to Nineveh. But Jonah's *calling*—what God wanted him to be—was to be a messenger of God's love.

Calling is about identity; it's about who you are.

It's a shift in thinking, isn't it? It's easy to think of your calling as a job description. Our cultural focus on doing and on basing our identity on our job or career tricks us into equating our calling with our activities. God's calling might include doing specific tasks, but the deeper intention is about identity.

Rest and Reconnect

In chapter 1, you contemplated this question: If your desire to please God with your work was more about *someone to be* and less about *something to do*, how might your life look different? Let's now reconsider this question.

Someone to be rather than something to do. I call this concept "spiritual vocation," which simply means a calling bigger than the self. We've seen that the Latin word for vocation means calling. The word "spiritual" means of the spirit or soul. Thus you get spiritual vocation.

The concept of spiritual vocation is actually quite simple, and it's something you can write out in a sentence or two. Here are a few examples: My spiritual vocation is...

to make things beautiful

to be a messenger of the love of Jesus

to protect and serve

to bring order to chaos

All these statements include the word "to," which implies an assignment. Yet the assignment is not a specific job. It is left open to allow God to shape the details. Just like the clouds.

Now it's your turn. What is your spiritual vocation? Answer in one simple sentence: My spiritual vocation is to...

If your calling were just about a job description, I think you'd get really bored. You would get discouraged, especially if the climate at your workplace was toxic or nonproductive. You'd feel tired all the time, and the meaning you once derived from work would fade.

Hmmm. Sounds like burnout, doesn't it?

When calling is about your identity rather than a task, you live and

work from that deeper place. It's never about what you accomplish,
or how you perform, or whether you succeed
financially. It's about having a deep security that
you are doing what you are supposed to do and
living the way God designed you to live. It's
from this place that you find meaning, and it
leads you to fulfillment.

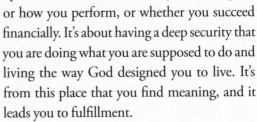

Calling is always about increasing connection with God and others.

Do you know what else? It's also a preventative measure for burnout.

Is It Time to Go?

One of the most frequent reasons people seek vocational counseling is to decide whether they should stay in a job or leave. Have you experienced this dilemma? It can provoke quite a bit of anxiety because you are unhappy in your current situation. Yet the unknown can sometimes bring greater fear—so much so that you become paralyzed or talk yourself out of the benefits of making a change.

I've found that this dilemma requires a matter-of-fact approach. Otherwise, the emotions and anxiety of the situation can swallow you. You may refuse to consciously decide, but of course, to not decide is still a decision. So why not decide the best route for you?

Basically, you have three options: suffer, cope, or quit.

Suffer

You may choose this option when you believe you have no other option. Perhaps you will retire soon and don't want to retool. You may need the paycheck. Perhaps your partner's job is local, and you don't have many other options. Whatever the issue, you feel you cannot leave.

Suffering is both an attitude and a decision—and it's not a great one. When you are suffering, your thoughts are negative. You aren't productive, and you may feel hopeless. Your attitude can rub off on others around you, which can affect your personal relationships and activities outside of work. It's a very powerless state of being. Because of that, I recommend that you look at the second option, which is coping.

Cope

You may choose this option when you have intentionally chosen to stay at your job and make the best of it. Coping is also an attitude and a decision—and it's a much more empowering one than suffering. Here are a few suggestions for coping:

- Do your personal work. Start with this book, particularly focusing on the exercises in chapters 7 through 10. You may also consider spiritual or professional counseling support.

- Get a support system in place. Develop relationships with positive people who replace your energy. Add meaningful activities outside of work, such as developing a new hobby.

- Renegotiate your expectations. Adjust to the real situation of your work and focus on what you can actually do versus what you want to do. Review chapter 7 for some tips.

Quit

You choose this option when you have no other option but to leave. Perhaps you want to advance your career or launch your own business. This is the riskiest and scariest decision, but you will know it is right for you when you feel peace in your heart. Let the Holy Spirit lead you, and seek wise counsel from people you trust.

Here's when you absolutely must leave a job:

- Your stress and burnout have impaired your entire life. Your physical health and personal relationships have suffered so much that you are in danger of losing something or someone permanently as a result.

- You have been chronically unhappy for a year or longer. You might think you are managing, or perhaps you've stayed because of your other life circumstances, like family security. However, I encourage you to consider a change. You have permission. This is not abundant life, and there are ways to make changes that are slow and don't uproot your family.

- Abusive or unethical things are happening at your job. God never asks you to stay in these situations. Get out.

When you feel exhausted and stuck at a job, the most limiting attitude you can have is to believe that you don't have any options. Do you remember Steve's story from chapter 4? He was able to make a move as soon as he shifted his perspective about his situation. You always have options. It's the feeling of powerlessness that keeps you stuck. When you realize the power you have to make choices, everything changes.

Women and Men

Do women and men experience calling differently? Women traditionally value nurturing and relationships, which is why the helping professions, such as teaching, social work, and nursing, often have more women workers. Men often find value in following duty or a purpose bigger than themselves. For men, sometimes it's enough to be connected to a value embedded in the work instead of the actual work. This is why men often engage in service work, such as transportation, food service, or middle management.

In chapter 10, you learned your values are directly related to your work satisfaction. Now that you've had some time to reflect, take a moment to write out the top five values you need to fulfill in your work.

You Are Called to Relationship

I wrote two chapters on calling because it's such an important topic. Calling is beautiful because you know that God has designed you for a special purpose and that he gave that purpose only to you. Then he asks you to step into that purpose (because it's always a choice on your part) and equips you to do the job he gives you. What an adventure that can be!

But for Christians, the concept of calling can potentially fuel a geyser of angst. Calling squeezes your heart and pinches your gut when you don't know it, or no longer feel it, or feel as if you are not living up to it. If you hear about calling in the church or even in your own spiritual practice, there can be an element of fear that you're not doing what you are supposed to do. That fear can be paralyzing—or worse, it can aggravate shame and depression. I believe those feelings are the root of burnout. That's why it's so important to bring this process to your awareness and to reflect on it deeply. I want you to find blessing and empowerment in your calling, not fear and exhaustion. And do you know what else? God does too.

Friend, please don't ever get down on yourself about your calling. You can never lose your calling, nor can you step outside of it. It comes from God, so it's way bigger than you; it's bigger than what your mind can imagine or your heart feels. If you ever feel you are not fulfilling your calling...well, that's literally impossible.

> You can never lose your calling or step outside of it.

Because your calling is never about what you do or don't do. It's about who you are in Jesus. And in that relationship, you naturally increase relationship and connection with others. You embody the love of Jesus. This is the one hope to which you have been called (Ephesians 4:4).

So get up today and go to work, or go about your day, knowing that you are right where you are supposed to be. Your burnout is unpleasant, but it's just part of your journey. It's going to teach you something about yourself and about God. You have permission to experience exactly what you are experiencing right now. You have permission to grow. You also have permission to move.

You are released to move in the direction that your heart leads, trusting the One who shaped that calling in your heart to begin with.

Chapter 14 Key Points

- Your calling is both fixed and fluid.
- Calling is someone to be, not something to do.
- You have permission to move.

Practice Being Released

Be still with the Holy Spirit. Remove any distractions that may be present. Sit or lie comfortably, close your eyes, and open your hands. Pray or meditate:

Holy Spirit, make my calling so very clear to me. Help me see who I am—who you want me to be—and not just what you want me to do. Give me the courage to live in this way, every day, for the rest of my life. I am released into further relationship, connection, and communion in the world, especially in the body of Christ.

Write, draw, sing, or otherwise express what God gives to you in these moments.

This Week's To-Be List

_____

_____

_____

_____

_____

_____

_____

_____

_____

_____

_____

_____

_____

_____

_____

_____

_____

15

Beautiful

He has made everything beautiful in its time.
ECCLESIASTES 3:11

The coils in the seat of your 1978 Chevy Blazer creak in delight as they bounce in rhythm to the jiggle of the car's old-school power steering. Barreling down the highway, there was no way you would miss that last pothole. It's almost as if you *had* to hit it because you knew this bad boy could handle it. It's just one of the joys of driving an old tank.

Literally, this tank is your joy. Lifted with Toyo tires and tinged turquoise, it's your baby. Well, really, it's your first love. It's what you learned to drive in. Years into your career, there came a day when you had enough extra to buy the one that would be all yours.

It's Friday morning, and your anticipation builds for the weekend ahead. Your favorite song is on the radio, and a travel mug holds your hot mojo, ready to fuel you through the morning. Because you're on your way to work.

Yeah, work.

It's been hard at work lately. You love what you do, but you haven't had that same satisfied feeling for a while. You're not totally sure why. Oh, you have some guesses. But sometimes it's easier not to think about it because you just have to get things done.

Stuck in your head, the song on the radio fades from your awareness as stress begins to rise in your body. You notice your heart pounding. Your nervous system has been hijacked, and you haven't even gotten to work yet!

But softly, sweetly, you begin to hear the most beautiful, angelic melody. The voices are not yours, but they feel so close, almost as if they are woven into you. They are coming from outside of you, but as you listen, you become aware that you are no longer listening with your ears. You are listening with your heart.

Something stirs your soul. Energy and joy weave themselves into a thread, drawing you into the song. The threads become a cord, drawing you further in, knitting you and them together, tighter, until you are all one chord. The song-colors are violet and beryl and light. Pure colors and transcendent, fashioning everything intensely beautiful.

From somewhere deep within, your song emerges. Your voice—the undercurrent, the harmony, or the overlay. It doesn't matter. Your voice blends perfectly with the others, and you sing at the top of your lungs. It's like you are a teenager again without a thought in the world except to be in this moment.

What if this song was what you were going to do today?

What if this song *was* your work?

Just like the threads that fashion that song, work is woven into your heart. It is such an important part of you. Yes, your work is a means of survival; your paycheck takes care of you and the people you love. But you and I both know that there is something deeper and much more meaningful about your work. Otherwise, you would not have gotten burned out...and you wouldn't have read this book.

God set it in the heart of humans to work (Genesis 2:15). Psychologically, you need to feel accomplishment and meaning, which is attained through work. You are called into vocation, which sets you apart from all the rest. Through your vocation, you come to God in a special relationship. It helps you understand your position with your Creator and assures you that you are loved and seen.

But when work fails to yield the meaning you once gained from it, your energy fades. You're going to need a lot more than your Chevy and a cup of mojo to get through this one.

A Beautiful Struggle

You are not alone in your struggle for meaning. King Solomon wrote the whole book of Ecclesiastes about the meaninglessness of work and life. Frankly, it is a rant that goes on and on and on. At the end of his rant, he basically throws up his hands and says that the only thing he knows for sure is to revere God and obey his commandments.

Imagine if this book had been a 15-chapter rant about the meaninglessness of work. You would be so depressed, and I would have been so depressed writing it!

I have good news for you. There is a beautiful resolution ahead.

> What do workers gain from their toil? I have seen the burden God has laid on the human race. He has made everything beautiful in its time. He has also set eternity in the human heart; yet no one can fathom what God has done from beginning to end (Ecclesiastes 3:9-11).

I love this passage. "He has made everything beautiful in its time" has been a hopeful statement for me during times of trial. I have learned that I can always count on God to redeem the painful, disastrous things of my life and transform them into something beautiful. But there is a deeper meaning about work in this passage—one that is not often noticed.

Solomon was talking about work here. He comes right out and says that God knows that work is difficult. God knows that the work he gave you sometimes can feel like a heavy burden. Otherwise, it wouldn't be work! But the burden that Solomon is referring to is also the meaning that you derive from work. Either you would be able to gain great meaning from work, or you wouldn't. The quest to make that meaning is the struggle.

But in the next breath, Solomon says God makes that struggle *beautiful in its time*. This is quite a statement from a man who struggled with meaning his whole life. The word "beauty" means something that is desirable or something that brings pleasure. Beauty is something that all humans, both men and women, seek as a point of satisfaction. It's not a term often used to describe work.

Have you ever considered that the goal of your work is to create beauty? In my years of career counseling, I've never had one conversation about it. But Solomon specifically used this term to describe the end result of his vocational struggle.

Here's the hopeful part: God transforms your struggle with work into something beautiful.

If you are a man, your work is likely about your sense of responsibility to provide for yourself and your family. The end goal of your work is to be valued and appreciated and to leave a legacy. It's cut and dried; your work is colorless. But you struggle with toil, and your meaning is often related to the perception of your personal success. Deep inside, you ache for beauty. Beauty brings color to your grayscale world because it's not something that you naturally have. Solomon is encouraging you that your work will never be in vain. Something good— something beautiful—will come out of it.

> God transforms your struggle with work into something beautiful.

If you are a woman, moving toward beauty feels natural. Women are wired to be beautiful and to make things beautiful. Solomon's words confirm a deep knowing for women that God values beauty. In your work, you know that whatever you produce or contribute is pleasing to God. You are affirmed that you are on the right path. You are allowed and encouraged to work because it puts forth beautiful things into the world.

Women and Men

What would it look like to move toward beauty in your work?

If you are a man, it means you are encouraged to move toward beauty. As a man, you probably don't really think about moving toward beauty at work. You just want to get the job done! You also may feel a little bit ashamed about your natural impulse toward beauty because of the energy it takes to manage your sexuality. But deep down, you need to know that what you do matters—that you are more than a body and a paycheck. Knowing that you matter helps you to connect beauty with work. How can you move toward beauty at work today?

- Reach out in relationship to a colleague. Offer to have coffee or write them an email of encouragement.
- Allow yourself to spend extra time on a work task or project that brings you satisfaction. When you have finished it, take some time to simply sit and enjoy it. Commend yourself with positive self-affirmation. *I did such a great job on this!*
- Save a little money from each paycheck to later spend on something that is meaningful to you.
- Catch yourself in a stressed or fatigued moment and simply stop. Give yourself five or ten relaxing deep breaths and close your eyes if you need to. Your body and mind will naturally restore a sense of balance.

If you are a woman, it means you are *allowed to embody beauty.* To embody something means to bring a nonphysical thing to physical form. You naturally embrace beauty, but in workplaces that often feel dominated by masculinity, sometimes it's difficult to allow your femininity to shine. How can you be the embodiment of beauty at work today?

- Spend extra time preparing yourself for work. This doesn't necessarily mean beautifying your physical appearance (although it could), but it might mean taking extra time in the morning to be still with God, taking a leisurely bath instead of a shower, or preparing a nice lunch on your best china.

- Create a work space that feels beautiful. Spend time and money on decor, photos, or tea to offer coworkers.
- As you approach each project or work task, consider: *How can this project become the embodiment of beauty?* You might be surprised at how it turns out!
- Sincerely compliment a colleague on a job well done.

Let Longing Be Your Teacher

I have been a seeker and I still am, but I stopped asking the books and the stars. I started listening to the teaching of my soul.

RUMI

Rumi was a thirteenth-century Sufi scholar, theologian, and poet. Much of his work focused on love and oneness, and his works are still enjoyed worldwide today. In Rumi's day, books represented education and science, and the stars (astrology) referred to spiritual thinking or religion. This quote is significant because Rumi is a learned and respected man who challenged the intellectual status quo by prioritizing the unpredictable path of the soul.

As you've learned in this book, your soul is the eternal part of you—the part that is separated from God in this existence with deep longing to return home. Fulfillment and meaning are two things that satiate the soul. Because your soul longs to return to oneness with God, it asks deep, existential questions. Seeking answers is a natural response to your soul's call.

You read this book because, like Rumi, you are a seeker.

On the surface, you may have been attracted to the cheerful cover and the promise to find a resolution to your burnout. Perhaps your boss or colleague gave you the book while you and your coworkers joked about how burned out you were. But deep down, something else prompted you to read this book. It was your longing, the quest of your soul.

Instead of fighting it, dismissing it, burying it, or numbing it, embrace longing as your teacher. Be still and listen to what it wants to teach you.

Your soul asks the questions. Don't ignore it, and don't forget to listen. Allow yourself to listen. Take the time off that you need to listen. Because the Voice in your heart and the knowing of your soul have the answers. He makes everything beautiful in its time.

The Meaning of Meaninglessness

King Solomon concluded that all work is meaningless, but I don't believe that. Many people experience meaninglessness in work, and just as many people experience meaninglessness in life. Unattended, it leads to burnout and depression. It's a sad state if you do not realize the bigger purpose behind it.

When you finally understand the meaning of meaninglessness, then everything just...makes...sense. (I laughed out loud after typing that line—the irony of "the meaning of meaninglessness" is hysterical!)

God allows meaninglessness and longing to move you toward the abundant life he dreamed for you. In that way, they are vehicles. Proverbs 25:2 says, "It is the glory of God to conceal a matter; to search out a matter is the glory of kings." In his all-knowing and all-seeing, God hides meaning as a treasure for you to discover. You are designed to pursue it.

It's hard to know what to pursue, though, when you feel defeated and tired. So I'll share something that God taught me. As a mental health counselor who specializes in trauma and vocational distress, I have borne witness to the deepest human pain and most horrific stories imaginable. Many years I struggled with finding joy and meaning in my work. Imagine my soul questions! I wrestled every day with the *why* and the *how* and the *what for.*

One day, the Holy Spirit whispered into my heart, "Amy, move toward beauty."

For every human emotion, there is an opposite. For depression, there is hope. For sadness, there is joy. For anxiety, there is peace. For confusion, there is truth. The antidote to the feeling that you don't want to feel is simply to move toward the feeling that you do.

> The treasure at the end of the pursuit of beauty is the meaning that your heart craves.

For pain, there is beauty.

God gave you the gift of beauty not only for your pleasure but also for your healing.

Rumi also said, "Let the beauty of what you love be what you do." It's easy to mistakenly think that beauty is a state that you attain. We fail to realize that beauty, like peace and fulfillment, is also a process—something you create and cultivate. Beauty is a soul experience; it is one of the most delightful fulfillments of longing. The treasure at the end of the pursuit of beauty is the meaning that your heart craves.

Pursue. Enjoy. Transcend.

You made it through the workweek. Whew! Now it's Saturday evening, and you're exhausted. Dirty sweat creases lines across your brow, and your thumb is bleeding from some kind of gash (you were so busy that you don't even remember how that happened). You sit on the edge of your deck and survey the scene:

A strand of ambient lights twinkle warmth as dusk steals the day. Smoke from the BBQ promises the imminent arrival of something delicious—right in time to fill your empty belly. You turn to greet your sweetie; they smile, hand you a cold drink, and begin to massage your shoulders.

It's the good kind of exhausted.

Your backyard is really taking shape. It was your design—your dream to create this space. All you. Every plant, every special touch was your idea. The colors and scents blend together perfectly; the restful trickle of a fountain refreshes your soul. It's like that song you heard driving to work yesterday. A dream formed by something outside of you, yet inviting you into it. And now, in this moment, your heart is full once again.

Enjoy it.

Enjoy it.

Did you enjoy the labor? Perhaps you did, but, quite honestly, you probably didn't. Like childbirth, you don't remember the pain it took to reach this moment, because the beauty of the moment transcends the pain of getting here. Whether it's your Chevy Blazer or that expensive designer blazer tailored just for you, the promise of future enjoyment moves you through toil. If you have ever wondered why you feel so compelled to work despite your struggle with work, it's because God designed labor as a mechanism to satisfaction.

I wrote "Enjoy it" twice back there because we somehow miss that part. Like a mortar and pestle, the culture's frenetic pace is ground into your mind from the first day of kindergarten. Go. Do. Achieve. I don't recall anyone ever teaching me "Pursue. Enjoy. Transcend." Yet in your work, that's the true bottom line. It's all so profound, so God, and so beautiful.

> God designed labor as a mechanism to satisfaction.

As you sit on your deck, you hear it—it *is* that same song from yesterday. It's the love-energy of God, singing over you. Only tonight his song doesn't fill you with fervor. Instead, its sweetness tenderly embraces you with the satisfaction of a job well done. I can almost see King Solomon sitting there beside you, raising his glass and smiling. *You finally understand. Yes, it's all meaningless...except for this. Enjoy!*

Friend, I hope you sit still in these beautiful moments. You've worked hard; breathe it all in. Savor every morsel. Open your heart to the Love that surrounds you, and...

...just be.

Chapter 15 Key Points

- God transforms your struggle with work into something beautiful.
- The pursuit of beauty creates meaning.
- Transcend burnout through the pursuit and enjoyment of work.

Practice Being with Beauty

Spend some time in a beautiful space. It can be in your home, outdoors, a church sanctuary, an art gallery, or anywhere else your heart is calling. Remove any distractions that may be present. Sit or lie comfortably, close your eyes, and open your hands. Pray or meditate:

God, I am still with you. Fill me with your beautiful presence. Teach me to enjoy the work of my hands.

This Week's To-Be List

_____

_____

_____

_____

_____

_____

_____

_____

_____

_____

_____

_____

_____

_____

_____

_____

_____

Afterword

Beyond Burnout

Be still, and know that I am God.

PSALM 46:10

When I was a little girl, I had a plaque with Psalm 46:10 printed it. My mother probably bought it at one of the many garage sales we frequented together. It was designed in the orange-and-olive drab that was so popular in the 1970s, and it had a picture of a little girl in a swamp looking at some ducks. It wasn't particularly pretty, but for some reason, my mother liked it and hung it in my room.

As a child, I didn't quite understand the meaning of the verse. Was the little girl actually being still if she was out exploring? Where was God? Why were there ducks in the picture instead of something a little more holy?

In college and during several adult transitions, I got rid of many childhood things. But I kept that plaque—probably because it was such an artifact of my heart. I recently pulled it out of storage when I was decorating my young daughter's room. I smiled, and the memories flooded my awareness.

Be still, and know that I am God. Like the plaque, this verse has been a garment folded up and packed into the boxes of my life. It was always pushed to the bottom; I never noticed it there or really held its relevance. That's how the human psyche is—familiarity becomes a thread of the mundane. Yet God's principles stay true, anticipating the moment your heart opens and unpacks.

As I hung that plaque on the wall, I was reminded that I don't practice stillness enough. I work long days and constantly feel overwhelmed; adding stillness to my to-do list doesn't get things done. But today, something beckoned me to put down the hammer.

Be still.

I took a breath and then exhaled all...the...things.

And I heard things I usually don't notice, like the birds chirping outside. More than the sweet song, I noticed their chirping flowed in rhythm and response, in a special bird language. I was a privy participant in their conversation. It was like a secret we shared, and I felt included. By birds. I felt included by birds. Wonderfully, it fostered a sense of belonging—as if I were right where I was supposed to be, loved, held, and accepted by the space around me. Right there, in my daughter's bedroom, I experienced God's immanence.

Be still, and know.

The quietness of the moment allowed my heart to open, channeling a pathway to the deepest part of my soul. My heart's defenses, forged through years of fatigue and disappointment, faded into a glow. The knowing part of me emerged—the part of my heart that is spacious with God's Spirit. I envisioned a taproot, sacred and sturdy. Without knowing how or why, I was overwhelmed with confidence that my next steps were God's leading toward my fulfillment.

Be still, and know that I am.

I rarely feel God's presence in my everyday activities...because I don't stop. In these moments, I did. I am—I exist—because I am connected to the great I AM. Yet my soul resides within a mortal body, with physical needs and limitations. It is my responsibility to meet those needs, with God's direction. In so doing, I honor both the mortal and immortal parts of me; I honor God.

Be still, and know that I am God.

My breath regulated. In and out, deeper and more rhythmic...and I remembered that there is order to everything. The great I AM is in control, and I can trust him. But I must choose to place my head to my Papa's chest; I must allow his order to blanket my chaos and just be held.

Belonging. Knowing. Stability. Comfort. All in five minutes of stillness.

I don't practice stillness enough. Do you?

It's not an accident that the Bible translators included a comma after *be still.* That comma is so very important because it makes you pause; that comma sanctions the simple as profound.

> Stillness is the prerequisite to restoration.

Because everything you seek comes after stillness; it is the pathway through your burnout and beyond. Stillness is the prerequisite to restoration.

As you set down this book and step forward into your life, this is the one big takeaway I most want to plant in your heart. Put it near the top of your toolkit, easily reached when needed. Consider it our farewell hug, along with my sincerest blessings for your future. It is this:

Wherever you go, and in all the great things you do, remember—simply be still.

The Five Intentions of Burnout Resolution

I.
I will practice stillness so God can
restore my soul.

II.
I will seek connection with God,
myself, and my work.

III.
I will cultivate awareness of who I am,
where I am, and what I want to be.

IV.
I will take consistent steps to
promote well-being in my work.

V.
I will focus on who I am to *be*,
not what I am to *do*.

Notes

Chapter 2: Be Longing

1. C.R. Snyder, *The Psychology of Hope: You Can Get There from Here* (New York: Free Press, 2003).

Chapter 3: Be Connected

1. D.J. Strümpfer, "Resilience and Burnout: A Stitch That Could Save Nine," *South African Journal of Psychology* 33 (2003): 69–79; Christina Maslach and Michael P. Leiter, *The Truth About Burnout: How Organizations Cause Personal Stress and What to Do About It* (San Francisco, CA: Jossey-Bass, 1997).

2. Paula Derrow, "Protect Yourself from Burnout," *Redbook* 225, no. 3 (2015): 116.

3. Abraham Maslow, *Toward a Psychology of Being* (Floyd, VA: Sublime Books, 2014). Originally published in 1962.

Chapter 4: Be Filled

1. Lexico, https://www.lexico.com/en/definition/calling.

2. Frank Parsons, *Choosing a Vocation* (London, UK: Gay and Hancock, 1909).

Chapter 5: Be Nourished

1. Vincent J. Fortunato and John Harsh, "Stress and Sleep Quality: The Moderating Role of Negative Affectivity," *Personality and Individual Differences* 41, no. 5 (2006): 825–36; Lynne J. Lamarche, Helen S. Driver, Geneviève Forest, and Joseph De Koninck, "Napping During the Late-Luteal Phase Improves Sleepiness, Alertness, Mood and Cognitive Performance in Women with and Without Premenstrual Symptoms," *Sleep and Biological Rhythms* 8, no. 2 (2010): 151–59.

2. R.L. Haupt, "Napping Improves Ethics," *IEEE Antennas and Propagation Magazine* 48, no. 3 (2006): 118; Jiwon Kim and Hyoung Ryoul Kim, "The Relationship Between Increased Job Stress and Weight Gain: A 2-Year Longitudinal Study," *Occupational and Environmental Medicine* 68, no. Suppl. 1 (2011): A76–A77; Sofia Klingberg, Kirsten Mehlig, Ingegerd Johansson, Bernt Lindahl, Anna Winkvist, and Lauren Lissner, "Occupational Stress Is Associated with Major Long-Term Weight Gain in a Swedish Population-Based Cohort," *International Archives of Occupational and Environmental Health* 92, no. 4 (2019): 569–76.

3. Jeffrey M. O'Brien, "Is Silicon Valley Bad for Your Health?," *Fortune* 172, no. 6 (2015): 154–162; Blair Johnson and Rebecca Acabchuk, "What Are the Keys to a Longer, Happier Life? Answers from Five Decades of Health Psychology Research," *Social Science & Medicine* 196 (2018): 218.

Chapter 7: Be Free

1. "Reinhold Niebuhr," Wikipedia, https://en.wikipedia.org/wiki/Reinhold_Niebuhr.

Chapter 9: Be Edified

1. Daniel Goleman, *Emotional Intelligence: Why It Can Matter More Than IQ* (New York: Bantam Books, 1995).

2. Aleksandra Jasielska, "Women's Career Success in a Man's Workplace—a Cross-National Study," *Romanian Journal of Experimental Applied Psychology* 5, no. 1 (2014): 23–32; Robert J. Taormina, "Helping Shy Employees with Career Success: The Impact of Organizational Socialization," *Psychological Thought* 12, no. 1 (2019): 41–62.

3. Graeme H. Coetzer, "Emotional Versus Cognitive Intelligence: Which Is the Better Predictor of Efficacy for Working in Teams?," *Journal of Behavioral & Applied Management* 16, no. 2 (2015): 116–33, http://search.ebscohost.com.ezproxy.proxy.library.oregonstate.edu/login.aspx?direct=true&db=aph&AN=134043109&site=ehost-live.

4. Sonia Mairaj Ahmad and Zainab Fotowwat Zadeh, "Gender Differences on the Variables of Emotional Intelligence, Creative-Potential, and Job Satisfaction in Managers," *Pakistan Journal of Psychology* 47, no. 2 (December 2016): 61–77, http://search.ebscohost.com.ezproxy.proxy.library.oregonstate.edu/login.aspx?direct=true&db=aph&AN=129038829&site=ehost-live.

5. Agneta H. Fischer, Mariska E. Kret, and Joost Broekens, "Gender Differences in Emotion Perception and Self-Reported Emotional Intelligence: A Test of the Emotion Sensitivity Hypothesis," *PLoS ONE* 13, no. 1 (2018): 1–19.

Chapter 10: Be Satisfied

1. Rosana Silvina Codaro, Patricia Amelia Tomei, and Bernardo Paraiso De Campos Serra, "Job Satisfaction and Career Choices: A Study Using Schein's Career Anchor Model," *Revista eletronica de estrategia e negocios* 10, no. 2 (2017): 3; Paul J. Hartung, "Cultural Context in Career Theory and Practice: Role Salience and Values," *Career Development Quarterly* 51, no. 1 (2002): 12–25.

About the Author

Amy O'Hana, PhD, is a licensed professional counselor and university professor. She specializes in helping people overcome adjustment, stress, grief, and trauma. She is the author of *When Your Child Is Grieving: God's Hope and Wisdom for the Journey Toward Healing.* Amy lives in the mountains of central Oregon and enjoys creating warm spaces, thinking deep thoughts, and engaging in coffee conversation with loved ones. Find her on the web at www.amyohana.com.

To learn more about Harvest House books and
to read sample chapters, visit our website:

www.harvesthousepublishers.com

HARVEST HOUSE PUBLISHERS
EUGENE, OREGON